Daily Skill Builders: Division

By

BARBARA ALLMAN, M.A.T.

ISBN 978-1-58037-443-9

Printing No. CD-404084

Mark Twain Media, Inc., Publishers
Distributed by Carson-Dellosa Publishing Company, Inc.

Table of Contents

Table of Contents (cont.)

Introduction to the Teacher

This edition of *Daily Skill Builders* is a powerful tool that will help you equip your students with a variety of important skills relating to division. Each half-page reproducible activity targets a specific skill, as shown in the Table of Contents. Tied to NCTM standards, these activities provide practice in basic division calculations.

The activities in this book will give your students daily practice with a variety of essential math skills. They are arranged so that each activity builds on the skills covered in the previous activities. You may use them in order, or use any section you need to reinforce your curriculum. Use the standards-correlation chart in the beginning of the book to locate problems on a specific skill.

When they complete the activities, students will be mastering skills such as division facts; dividing numbers from one to five digits with and without remainders; dividing by multiples of 10; estimating; averages; greatest common factors; prime factors; problem solving with division; dividing decimals; reducing fractions with division; dividing fractions, mixed numbers, and whole numbers; finding percents; and divisibility rules.

We hope you and your students find these exercises both useful and engaging. Division is an integral part of performing higher math skills and achieving higher test scores. These *Daily Skill Builders* are designed to help your students hone their math skills to razor sharpness.

In short, use these *Daily Skill Builders* any and every way you can to make the most of all the tools packed inside. Expect your students' division skills to grow throughout the year!

NCTM Standards Correlation

Number and Operations Standard (Grades 3–5)	Activities
Understand numbers, ways of representing numbers, relationships among numbers, and number systems.	
• Understand the place-value structure of the base-ten number system and be able to represent and compare whole numbers and decimals.	61, 62
• Recognize and generate equivalent forms of commonly used fractions, decimals, and percents.	105, 106, 107, 108
Understand meanings of operations and how they relate to one another.	
• Understand various meanings of multiplication and division.	7, 8
• Understand the effects of multiplying and dividing whole numbers.	79, 80
• Identify and use relationships between operations, such as division as the inverse of multiplication, to solve problems.	9, 10, 57, 58, 59, 60
• Describe classes of numbers according to characteristics, such as the nature of their factors.	139, 140, 141, 142, 143, 144, 145, 146, 147, 148, 149, 150, 151, 152, 153, 154, 155, 156, 157, 158, 159, 160
Compute fluently and make reasonable estimates.	
• Develop fluency with basic number combinations for multiplication and division, and use these combinations to mentally compute related problems, such as 30 x 50.	39, 40, 41, 42, 43, 44
• Develop fluency in adding, subtracting, multiplying, and dividing whole numbers.	11, 12, 13, 14, 15, 16, 17, 18, 19, 20, 21, 22, 23, 24, 25, 26, 27, 28, 29, 30, 31, 32, 33, 34, 35, 36, 37, 38, 45, 46, 47, 48, 49, 50, 51, 52, 77, 78
• Develop and use strategies to estimate the results of whole-number computations and to judge the reasonableness of such results.	53, 54, 55, 56

NCTM Standards Correlation (cont.)

Number and Operations Standard (Grades 6–8)	Activities
Understand numbers, ways of representing numbers, relationships among numbers, and number systems.	
• Work flexibly with fractions, decimals, and percents to solve problems.	133, 134, 135, 136, 137, 138
• Use factors, multiples, prime factorization, and relatively prime numbers to solve problems.	69, 70, 71, 72, 73, 74, 75, 76
Understand meanings of operations and how they relate to one another.	
• Understand and use the inverse relationships of addition and subtraction, multiplication and division, and squaring and finding square roots to simplify computations and solve problems.	57, 58, 59, 60
Compute fluently and make reasonable estimates.	
• Select appropriate methods and tools for computing with fractions and decimals from among mental computation, estimation, calculators or computers, and paper and pencil, depending on the situation, and apply selected methods.	67, 68
• Develop and analyze algorithms for computing with fractions, decimals, and integers and develop fluency in their use.	93, 94, 95, 96, 97, 98, 99, 100, 101, 102, 103, 104, 105, 106, 107, 108, 109, 110, 111, 112, 113, 114, 115, 116, 117, 118, 119, 120, 121, 122, 123, 124, 125, 126, 127, 128, 129, 130, 131, 132
Data Analysis and Probability Standard (Grades 6–8)	
Select and use appropriate statistical methods to analyze data.	
• Find, use, and interpret measures of center and spread, including mean and interquartile range.	63, 64, 65, 66
Problem Solving Standard (Grades 3–5 and 6–8)	
• Solve problems that arise in mathematics and in other contexts.	81, 82, 83, 84, 85, 86, 87, 88, 89, 90, 91, 92

ACTIVITY 1 About Division

Name: ______________________

Date: ______________________

Division is the reverse of multiplication. In division, a number is separated into equal groups of smaller numbers.

Divide.

1. Tayla drew a colorful design with geometric figures. Each figure had three sides. The total number of sides was 180. How many figures did Tayla draw? ______________

2. Tayla used six colors in her design: green, yellow, red, blue, orange, and purple. Half of the figures were green. How many figures was that? ______________

3. Tayla colored the remaining figures so there would be the same number of red, blue, orange, purple, and yellow. How many of each of those colors did Tayla make? ______________

4. If Tayla had used only green, red, and yellow in her design, and half were green, how many would she have made of each of the other two colors? ______________

ACTIVITY 2 Division Terms

Name: ______________________

Date: ______________________

$56 \div 8 = 7$

A **dividend** is a number to be divided by another number. In the example division problem, 56 is the dividend.
A **divisor** is the number by which another number is divided. The divisor is 8.
A **quotient** is the answer in a division problem. The quotient is 7.

1. $820 \div 20 = 41$ What is the dividend? __________
   What is the divisor? __________ What is the quotient? __________
2. $3,708 \div 6 = 618$ What is the dividend? __________
   What is the divisor? __________ What is the quotient? __________
3. $1,450 \div 5 = 290$ What is the dividend? __________
   What is the divisor? __________ What is the quotient? __________
4. $10\overline{)400}$ with quotient 40 What is the dividend? __________
   What is the divisor? __________ What is the quotient? __________
5. $25\overline{)75}$ with quotient 3 What is the dividend? __________
   What is the divisor? __________ What is the quotient? __________

ACTIVITY 3 Remainder

Name: ______________________

Date: ______________________

A **remainder** is the number left over in the quotient of a division problem. In the example problem, the remainder is 1.

$43 \div 7 = 6\ r\,1$

Divide. Write the quotient and the remainder.

1. **a.** $93 \div 10 =$ ______________ **b.** $17 \div 5 =$ ______________

c. $46 \div 9 =$ ______________ **d.** $303 \div 10 =$ ______________

Review. $79 \div 7 = 11\ r\,2$

2. Circle the dividend.

3. Underline the divisor.

4. Draw a box around the quotient.

5. What is the remainder? ______________

ACTIVITY 4 Review

Name: ______________________

Date: ______________________

Fill in the blanks.

remainder **quotient** **opposite** **divisor** **dividend** **equal** **division**

1. The number that is the answer in a division problem. ______________________
2. A number to be divided by another number. ______________________
3. The number left over in the quotient of a division problem. ______________________
4. The number by which another number is divided. ______________________
5. The reverse of multiplication. ______________________
6. In division, a number is separated into ______________________ groups.
7. Division is the ______________________ of multiplication.
8. Explain how three friends can share a dozen apple slices.

____

____

9. Write and solve a division word problem about you and your friends.

____

____

ACTIVITY 5 It's a Fact

Name:____________________

Date:____________________

Fill in the multiplication table.

6												
5												
4												
3												
2												
1												
	1	2	3	4	5	6	7	8	9	10	11	12

Solve each division problem. Check your answers using the table.

1. 20 ÷ 5 = __________
2. 12 ÷ 4 = __________
3. 50 ÷ 5 = __________
4. 18 ÷ 6 = __________
5. 9 ÷ 3 = __________
6. 27 ÷ 3 = __________
7. 33 ÷ 11 = __________
8. 15 ÷ 3 = __________
9. 36 ÷ 6 = __________
10. 11 ÷ 1 = __________
11. 54 ÷ 9 = __________
12. 30 ÷ 5 = __________
13. 44 ÷ 4 = __________
14. 60 ÷ 5 = __________
15. 27 ÷ 3 = __________

ACTIVITY 6 Further Facts

Name:____________________

Date:____________________

Fill in the multiplication table.

12												
11												
10												
9												
8												
7												
	1	2	3	4	5	6	7	8	9	10	11	12

Solve each division problem. Check your answers using the table.

1. 70 ÷ 10 = __________
2. 63 ÷ 7 = __________
3. 81 ÷ 9 = __________
4. 14 ÷ 2 = __________
5. 44 ÷ 4 = __________
6. 55 ÷ 11 = __________
7. 108 ÷ 12 = __________
8. 99 ÷ 9 = __________
9. 144 ÷ 12 = __________
10. 121 ÷ 11 = __________
11. 64 ÷ 8 = __________
12. 110 ÷ 10 = __________
13. 32 ÷ 4 = __________
14. 35 ÷ 7 = __________
15. 132 ÷ 11 = __________

ACTIVITY 7 That's a Fact

Name: ____________________

Date: ____________________

A fact family shows how division and multiplication are related. For example:

8 x 7 = 56
7 x 8 = 56
56 ÷ 8 = 7
56 ÷ 7 = 8

Complete each fact family.

1. 2 x 8 = 16
_____ x 2 = 16
16 ÷ 8 = _____
_____ ÷ 2 = 8

2. 4 x 6 = 24
_____ x 4 = 24
24 ÷ 6 = _____
_____ ÷ 4 = 6

3. 12 x 9 = 108
_____ x 12 = 108
108 ÷ 9 = _____
_____ ÷ 12 = 9

4. 10 x 5 = 50
_____ x 10 = 50
50 ÷ 5 = _____
_____ ÷ 10 = 5

5. 7 x 4 = 28
_____ x 7 = 28
28 ÷ 4 = _____
_____ ÷ 7 = 4

6. 8 x 3 = 24
_____ x 8 = 24
24 ÷ 3 = _____
_____ ÷ 8 = 3

7. 2 x 9 = 18
_____ x 2 = 18
18 ÷ 9 = _____
_____ ÷ 2 = 9

8. 11 x 10 = 110
_____ x 11 = 110
110 ÷ 10 = _____
_____ ÷ 11 = 10

9. 8 x 8 = 64
_____ x 8 = 64
64 ÷ 8 = _____
_____ ÷ 8 = 8

ACTIVITY 8 Is That a Fact?

Name: ____________________

Date: ____________________

A fact family shows how division and multiplication are related. For example:

5 x 7 = 35
7 x 5 = 35
35 ÷ 7 = 5
35 ÷ 5 = 7

Complete each fact family.

1. 9 x 8 = 72
_____ x 9 = 72
72 ÷ 8 = _____
_____ ÷ 9 = 8

2. 7 x 7 = 49
_____ x 7 = 49
49 ÷ 7 = _____
_____ ÷ 7 = 7

3. 12 x 2 = 24
_____ x 12 = 24
24 ÷ 2 = _____
_____ ÷ 12 = 2

4. 11 x 12 = 132
_____ x 11 = 132
132 ÷ 12 = _____
_____ ÷ 11 = 12

5. 9 x 4 = 36
_____ x 9 = 36
36 ÷ 4 = _____
_____ ÷ 9 = 4

6. 5 x 9 = 45
_____ x 5 = 45
45 ÷ 9 = _____
_____ ÷ 5 = 9

7. 4 x 3 = 12
_____ x 4 = 12
12 ÷ 3 = _____
_____ ÷ 4 = 3

8. 6 x 8 = 48
_____ x 6 = 48
48 ÷ 8 = _____
_____ ÷ 6 = 8

9. 4 x 5 = 20
_____ x 4 = 20
20 ÷ 5 = _____
_____ ÷ 4 = 5

ACTIVITY 9 Fruitful Facts

Name: ____________________

Date: ____________________

Use all the numbers in each box to make a division fact.
The first one is done for you

1. 35 ÷ 7 = 5

3	7
5	5

2. ____ ÷ ____ = ____

3	4
1	2

3. ____ ÷ ____ = ____

3	6
0	5

4. ____ ÷ ____ = ____

5	6
9	4

5. ____ ÷ ____ = ____

1	4
7	2

6. ____ ÷ ____ = ____

8	4
5	0

ACTIVITY 10 Juggling Facts

Name: ____________________

Date: ____________________

Use all the numbers in the boxes to make a division fact.
The first one is done for you

1. 18 ÷ 6 = 3

3	6
8	1

2. ____ ÷ ____ = ____

3	7
1	2

3. ____ ÷ ____ = ____

7	4
8	2

4. ____ ÷ ____ = ____

9	4
7	7

5. ____ ÷ ____ = ____

5	4
5	9

6. ____ ÷ ____ = ____

3	4
8	2

ACTIVITY 11 Just Peachy

Name: ____________________

Date: ____________________

16 ÷ 4 = 4

Divide.

1. 40 ÷ 8 = ________
2. 72 ÷ 9 = ________
3. 18 ÷ 3 = ________
4. 36 ÷ 9 = ________
5. 44 ÷ 4 = ________
6. 48 ÷ 4 = ________
7. 35 ÷ 5 = ________
8. 20 ÷ 4 = ________

9. 54 ÷ 6 = ________
10. 21 ÷ 7 = ________
11. 24 ÷ 3 = ________
12. 63 ÷ 9 = ________
13. 99 ÷ 9 = ________
14. 32 ÷ 4 = ________
15. 16 ÷ 2 = ________
16. 30 ÷ 3 = ________

ACTIVITY 12 How Corny

Name: ____________________

Date: ____________________

20 ÷ 5 = 4

Divide.

1. 25 ÷ 5 = ________
2. 12 ÷ 6 = ________
3. 77 ÷ 7 = ________
4. 64 ÷ 8 = ________
5. 45 ÷ 9 = ________
6. 60 ÷ 5 = ________
7. 33 ÷ 3 = ________
8. 28 ÷ 7 = ________

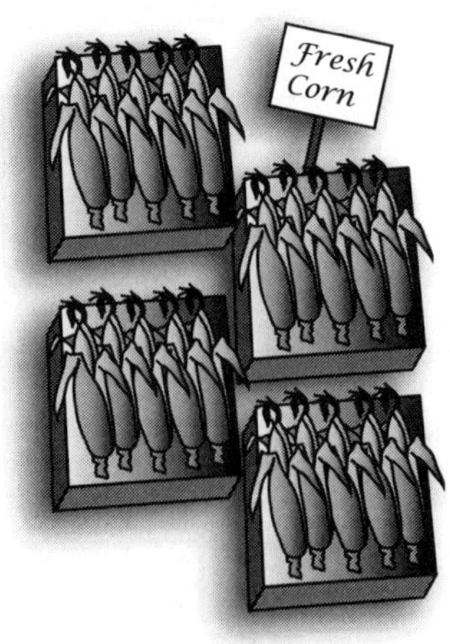

9. 50 ÷ 5 = ________
10. 56 ÷ 7 = ________
11. 42 ÷ 6 = ________
12. 48 ÷ 8 = ________
13. 72 ÷ 6 = ________
14. 32 ÷ 4 = ________
15. 15 ÷ 5 = ________
16. 84 ÷ 7 = ________

ACTIVITY 13 Berry Sweet

Name: ____________________

Date: ____________________

$25 \div 6 = 4\ r\,1$

Divide. Write the quotient and remainder.

1. $61 \div 6 =$ ____________
2. $30 \div 7 =$ ____________
3. $43 \div 6 =$ ____________
4. $74 \div 9 =$ ____________
5. $55 \div 6 =$ ____________
6. $50 \div 4 =$ ____________
7. $73 \div 6 =$ ____________
8. $16 \div 5 =$ ____________

9. $33 \div 6 =$ ____________
10. $38 \div 4 =$ ____________
11. $22 \div 3 =$ ____________
12. $19 \div 8 =$ ____________
13. $11 \div 2 =$ ____________
14. $37 \div 7 =$ ____________
15. $25 \div 8 =$ ____________
16. $19 \div 3 =$ ____________

ACTIVITY 14 Squash It

Name: ____________________

Date: ____________________

$11 \div 3 = 3\ r\,2$

Divide. Write the quotient and remainder.

1. $15 \div 7 =$ ____________
2. $43 \div 6 =$ ____________
3. $17 \div 2 =$ ____________
4. $68 \div 6 =$ ____________
5. $58 \div 8 =$ ____________
6. $22 \div 5 =$ ____________
7. $53 \div 5 =$ ____________
8. $25 \div 8 =$ ____________

9. $67 \div 6 =$ ____________
10. $36 \div 7 =$ ____________
11. $44 \div 6 =$ ____________
12. $16 \div 7 =$ ____________
13. $37 \div 3 =$ ____________
14. $31 \div 5 =$ ____________
15. $55 \div 6 =$ ____________
16. $29 \div 3 =$ ____________

ACTIVITY 15 Cherry Red

Name: ____________________

Date: ____________________

15 ÷ 7 = 2 *r* 1

Divide. Some have remainders!

1. 37 ÷ 6 = __________
2. 42 ÷ 7 = __________
3. 16 ÷ 6 = __________
4. 57 ÷ 9 = __________
5. 41 ÷ 8 = __________
6. 28 ÷ 7 = __________
7. 60 ÷ 6 = __________
8. 52 ÷ 3 = __________

9. 22 ÷ 4 = __________
10. 40 ÷ 8 = __________
11. 65 ÷ 4 = __________
12. 19 ÷ 2 = __________
13. 88 ÷ 8 = __________
14. 49 ÷ 3 = __________
15. 23 ÷ 4 = __________
16. 26 ÷ 5 = __________

ACTIVITY 16 Peas in a Pod

Name: ____________________

Date: ____________________

21 ÷ 4 = 5 *r* 1

Divide. Some have remainders!

1. 24 ÷ 3 = __________
2. 24 ÷ 5 = __________
3. 70 ÷ 7 = __________
4. 96 ÷ 8 = __________
5. 38 ÷ 6 = __________
6. 59 ÷ 7 = __________
7. 35 ÷ 5 = __________
8. 62 ÷ 6 = __________

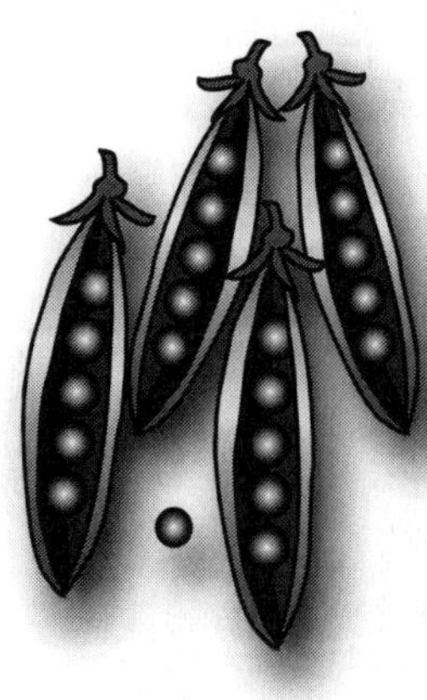

9. 80 ÷ 4 = __________
10. 95 ÷ 7 = __________
11. 50 ÷ 2 = __________
12. 27 ÷ 3 = __________
13. 75 ÷ 4 = __________
14. 67 ÷ 3 = __________
15. 36 ÷ 3 = __________
16. 85 ÷ 4 = __________

ACTIVITY 17 Building Skill

Name: ____________________

Date: ____________________

200 ÷ 5 = 40

Divide.

1. 312 ÷ 6 = ________

2. 350 ÷ 7 = ________

3. 150 ÷ 6 = ________

4. 900 ÷ 9 = ________

5. 504 ÷ 8 = ________

6. 364 ÷ 7 = ________

7. 294 ÷ 6 = ________

8. 231 ÷ 3 = ________

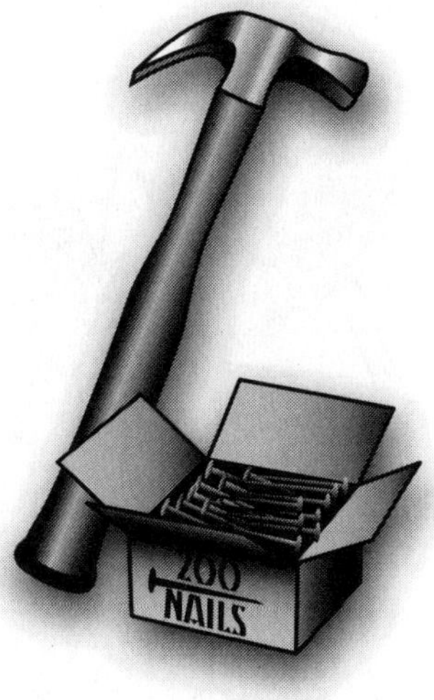

9. 480 ÷ 4 = ________

10. 400 ÷ 8 = ________

11. 220 ÷ 4 = ________

12. 190 ÷ 2 = ________

13. 112 ÷ 8 = ________

14. 273 ÷ 3 = ________

15. 852 ÷ 6 = ________

16. 385 ÷ 5 = ________

ACTIVITY 18 Tools of the Trade

Name: ____________________

Date: ____________________

Fill in the circle of the number that completes each equation.

		a.	b.	c.	d.
1.	175 ÷ 5 = ____	53	35	17	31
2.	336 ÷ 6 = ____	36	46	56	66
3.	222 ÷ 3 = ____	74	174	64	72
4.	156 ÷ ____ = 39	3	4	5	6
5.	385 ÷ ____ = 55	4	5	6	7
6.	318 ÷ ____ = 159	2	3	4	5

ACTIVITY 19 Construction Zone

Name: ______________________

Date: ______________________

$127 \div 2 = 63\ r\ 1$

Divide.

1. $329 \div 8 =$ ____________
2. $415 \div 7 =$ ____________
3. $253 \div 5 =$ ____________
4. $809 \div 9 =$ ____________
5. $323 \div 4 =$ ____________
6. $366 \div 4 =$ ____________
7. $275 \div 6 =$ ____________
8. $861 \div 2 =$ ____________

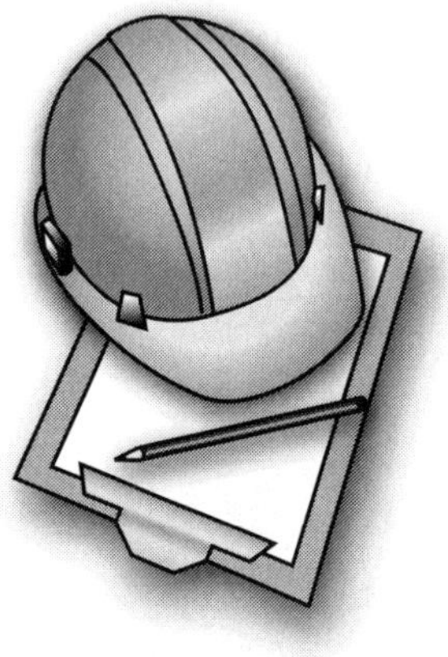

9. $413 \div 4 =$ ____________
10. $187 \div 8 =$ ____________
11. $220 \div 7 =$ ____________
12. $147 \div 2 =$ ____________
13. $489 \div 8 =$ ____________
14. $167 \div 3 =$ ____________
15. $758 \div 6 =$ ____________
16. $312 \div 5 =$ ____________

ACTIVITY 20 Under Construction

Name: ______________________

Date: ______________________

Fill in the circle of the number that completes each equation.

		a.	b.	c.	d.
1.	$215 \div 3 =$ ____	72 *r* 1	73 *r* 2	71 *r* 1	71 *r* 2
2.	$227 \div 5 =$ ____	45 *r* 2	46 *r* 1	45 *r* 1	46 *r* 2
3.	$373 \div 4 =$ ____	83 *r* 1	83 *r* 4	93 *r* 1	91 *r* 3
4.	$365 \div$ ____ $= 52\ r\ 1$	5	6	7	8
5.	$199 \div$ ____ $= 22\ r\ 1$	6	7	8	9
6.	$764 \div$ ____ $= 95\ r\ 4$	2	4	8	9

ACTIVITY 21 Construction Business

Name: ____________________

Date: ____________________

Divide. Some have remainders!

1. 393 ÷ 5 = __________
2. 729 ÷ 9 = __________
3. 360 ÷ 4 = __________
4. 357 ÷ 4 = __________
5. 175 ÷ 7 = __________
6. 999 ÷ 6 = __________
7. 511 ÷ 3 = __________
8. 804 ÷ 2 = __________
9. 155 ÷ 8 = __________
10. 410 ÷ 5 = __________
11. 515 ÷ 9 = __________
12. 196 ÷ 7 = __________
13. 223 ÷ 6 = __________
14. 195 ÷ 8 = __________
15. 147 ÷ 3 = __________
16. 144 ÷ 2 = __________

ACTIVITY 22 Construction Crew

Name: ____________________

Date: ____________________

Divide. Some have remainders!

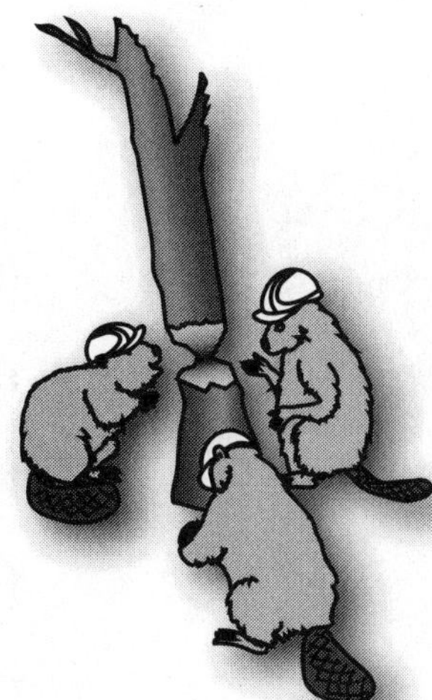

1. 487 ÷ 9 = __________
2. 131 ÷ 2 = __________
3. 486 ÷ 6 = __________
4. 355 ÷ 5 = __________
5. 247 ÷ 7 = __________
6. 357 ÷ 7 = __________
7. 274 ÷ 4 = __________
8. 184 ÷ 8 = __________
9. 139 ÷ 3 = __________
10. 280 ÷ 9 = __________
11. 165 ÷ 5 = __________
12. 278 ÷ 4 = __________
13. 201 ÷ 3 = __________
14. 313 ÷ 8 = __________
15. 330 ÷ 6 = __________
16. 177 ÷ 2 = __________

ACTIVITY 23 Pound Puppy

Name: ____________________

Date: ____________________

Divide.

1. 2,034 ÷ 6 = __________
2. 2,464 ÷ 7 = __________
3. 4,938 ÷ 6 = __________
4. 4,707 ÷ 9 = __________
5. 5,048 ÷ 8 = __________
6. 1,477 ÷ 7 = __________
7. 3,685 ÷ 5 = __________
8. 1,584 ÷ 3 = __________

9. 5,888 ÷ 4 = __________
10. 4,168 ÷ 8 = __________
11. 2,740 ÷ 4 = __________
12. 5,638 ÷ 2 = __________
13. 6,480 ÷ 8 = __________
14. 2,550 ÷ 3 = __________
15. 4,338 ÷ 6 = __________
16. 1,275 ÷ 5 = __________

ACTIVITY 24 Cat's Meow

Name: ____________________

Date: ____________________

Divide.

1. 1,767 ÷ 3 = __________
2. 2,128 ÷ 4 = __________
3. 1,548 ÷ 6 = __________
4. 2,060 ÷ 5 = __________
5. 1,806 ÷ 7 = __________
6. 1,926 ÷ 2 = __________
7. 3,213 ÷ 9 = __________
8. 2,856 ÷ 8 = __________

9. 1,431 ÷ 9 = __________
10. 6,450 ÷ 5 = __________
11. 1,428 ÷ 4 = __________
12. 1,308 ÷ 2 = __________
13. 6,027 ÷ 7 = __________
14. 2,094 ÷ 3 = __________
15. 5,172 ÷ 6 = __________
16. 1,578 ÷ 2 = __________

ACTIVITY 25 Bunny Hop

Name: ____________________

Date: ____________________

2,144 ÷ 6 = 357 *r* 2

Divide.

1. 2,047 ÷ 3 = __________
2. 2,569 ÷ 8 = __________
3. 1,418 ÷ 4 = __________
4. 9,333 ÷ 8 = __________
5. 1,763 ÷ 5 = __________
6. 2,054 ÷ 7 = __________
7. 3,277 ÷ 6 = __________
8. 2,955 ÷ 9 = __________

9. 8,074 ÷ 9 = __________
10. 9,123 ÷ 2 = __________
11. 4,139 ÷ 7 = __________
12. 1,925 ÷ 3 = __________
13. 1,798 ÷ 5 = __________
14. 1,535 ÷ 7 = __________
15. 5,306 ÷ 8 = __________
16. 3,729 ÷ 6 = __________

ACTIVITY 26 Turtle Time

Name: ____________________

Date: ____________________

Fill in the circle of the number that completes each equation.

		a.	b.	c.	d.
1.	4,007 ÷ 5 = _____	701 *r* 2	810 *r* 2	801 *r* 3	801 *r* 2
2.	4,220 ÷ 6 = _____	660 *r* 2	703 *r* 1	703 *r* 2	803 *r* 2
3.	3,174 ÷ 7 = _____	453 *r* 3	443 *r* 3	443 *r* 2	462 *r* 1
4.	5,287 ÷ _____ = 881 *r* 1	4	6	8	9
5.	1,950 ÷ _____ = 487 *r* 2	2	4	6	7
6.	7,520 ÷ _____ = 835 *r* 5	3	5	7	9

ACTIVITY 27 Pretty Bird

Name: ______________________

Date: ______________________

Divide. Some have remainders!

1. 1,702 ÷ 3 = __________
2. 1,585 ÷ 5 = __________
3. 5,066 ÷ 8 = __________
4. 6,923 ÷ 7 = __________
5. 1,268 ÷ 2 = __________
6. 9,452 ÷ 9 = __________
7. 1,509 ÷ 3 = __________
8. 3,609 ÷ 4 = __________

9. 2,703 ÷ 6 = __________
10. 2,033 ÷ 5 = __________
11. 1,660 ÷ 2 = __________
12. 3,042 ÷ 4 = __________
13. 5,965 ÷ 7 = __________
14. 5,520 ÷ 8 = __________
15. 6,327 ÷ 3 = __________
16. 4,533 ÷ 9 = __________

ACTIVITY 28 Favorite Fish

Name: ______________________

Date: ______________________

Divide. Some have remainders!

1. 4,520 ÷ 8 = __________
2. 5,637 ÷ 7 = __________
3. 4,865 ÷ 5 = __________
4. 9,224 ÷ 8 = __________
5. 5,496 ÷ 3 = __________
6. 5,114 ÷ 6 = __________
7. 7,295 ÷ 7 = __________
8. 1,005 ÷ 2 = __________

9. 2,680 ÷ 4 = __________
10. 1,354 ÷ 5 = __________
11. 2,409 ÷ 3 = __________
12. 2,955 ÷ 9 = __________
13. 1,759 ÷ 7 = __________
14. 1,968 ÷ 6 = __________
15. 1,590 ÷ 4 = __________
16. 3,663 ÷ 9 = __________

ACTIVITY 29 A Rose Is a Rose

Name: ____________________

Date: ____________________

Divide.

1. 21,063 ÷ 3 = __________
2. 34,355 ÷ 5 = __________
3. 15,704 ÷ 2 = __________
4. 74,008 ÷ 8 = __________
5. 41,155 ÷ 5 = __________
6. 84,320 ÷ 4 = __________
7. 12,042 ÷ 6 = __________
8. 49,386 ÷ 6 = __________
9. 26,240 ÷ 8 = __________
10. 27,243 ÷ 9 = __________
11. 49,280 ÷ 7 = __________
12. 17,499 ÷ 3 = __________
13. 15,884 ÷ 4 = __________
14. 17,532 ÷ 9 = __________
15. 36,470 ÷ 7 = __________
16. 14,796 ÷ 2 = __________

ACTIVITY 30 Tiptoe Through the Tulips

Name: ____________________

Date: ____________________

Divide.

1. 30,175 ÷ 5 = __________
2. 27,200 ÷ 8 = __________
3. 22,402 ÷ 2 = __________
4. 90,210 ÷ 3 = __________
5. 87,768 ÷ 9 = __________
6. 56,084 ÷ 7 = __________
7. 33,705 ÷ 5 = __________
8. 63,040 ÷ 8 = __________
9. 17,496 ÷ 3 = __________
10. 11,444 ÷ 4 = __________
11. 29,316 ÷ 4 = __________
12. 36,792 ÷ 9 = __________
13. 15,400 ÷ 2 = __________
14. 23,220 ÷ 6 = __________
15. 34,818 ÷ 6 = __________
16. 38,451 ÷ 7 = __________

ACTIVITY 31 Forget-Me-Not

Name: ____________________

Date: ____________________

Divide. Write the quotient and the remainder.

1. 78,210 ÷ 7 = __________
2. 46,971 ÷ 5 = __________
3. 64,219 ÷ 3 = __________
4. 85,204 ÷ 9 = __________
5. 56,732 ÷ 8 = __________
6. 28,691 ÷ 6 = __________
7. 63,821 ÷ 4 = __________
8. 71,829 ÷ 2 = __________

9. 14,789 ÷ 9 = __________
10. 89,632 ÷ 7 = __________
11. 63,214 ÷ 5 = __________
12. 21,478 ÷ 3 = __________
13. 74,123 ÷ 8 = __________
14. 30,741 ÷ 6 = __________
15. 52,369 ÷ 4 = __________
16. 54,713 ÷ 2 = __________

ACTIVITY 32 Daisy Do

Name: ____________________

Date: ____________________

Divide. Be sure to write the quotient and the remainder.

1. 86,321 ÷ 2 = __________
2. 56,783 ÷ 4 = __________
3. 82,743 ÷ 6 = __________
4. 23,507 ÷ 8 = __________
5. 10,507 ÷ 3 = __________
6. 21,706 ÷ 5 = __________
7. 40,235 ÷ 7 = __________
8. 37,608 ÷ 9 = __________

9. 75,311 ÷ 2 = __________
10. 52,037 ÷ 4 = __________
11. 73,102 ÷ 6 = __________
12. 45,300 ÷ 8 = __________
13. 83,342 ÷ 3 = __________
14. 23,177 ÷ 5 = __________
15. 52,069 ÷ 7 = __________
16. 20,553 ÷ 9 = __________

ACTIVITY 33 Bird of Paradise

Name: ____________________

Date: ____________________

Divide. Some have remainders!

1. 45,098 ÷ 4 = __________
2. 60,288 ÷ 9 = __________
3. 80,714 ÷ 5 = __________
4. 16,203 ÷ 3 = __________
5. 94,466 ÷ 2 = __________
6. 21,548 ÷ 4 = __________
7. 16,505 ÷ 8 = __________
8. 10,150 ÷ 7 = __________

9. 32,772 ÷ 6 = __________
10. 14,072 ÷ 2 = __________
11. 64,977 ÷ 5 = __________
12. 64,072 ÷ 7 = __________
13. 67,800 ÷ 3 = __________
14. 24,831 ÷ 6 = __________
15. 22,424 ÷ 8 = __________
16. 20,745 ÷ 9 = __________

ACTIVITY 34 Morning Glory

Name: ____________________

Date: ____________________

Divide. Some have remainders!

1. 83,502 ÷ 3 = __________
2. 14,280 ÷ 6 = __________
3. 47,074 ÷ 9 = __________
4. 73,982 ÷ 2 = __________
5. 12,174 ÷ 3 = __________
6. 75,304 ÷ 5 = __________
7. 21,196 ÷ 7 = __________
8. 39,710 ÷ 8 = __________

9. 44,707 ÷ 9 = __________
10. 36,596 ÷ 7 = __________
11. 13,146 ÷ 2 = __________
12. 15,931 ÷ 5 = __________
13. 23,310 ÷ 6 = __________
14. 27,784 ÷ 8 = __________
15. 30,124 ÷ 4 = __________
16. 25,289 ÷ 4 = __________

ACTIVITY 35 Two by Two

Name: ______________________

Date: ______________________

Divide.

1. 165 ÷ 3 = __________
2. 485 ÷ 5 = __________
3. 392 ÷ 7 = __________
4. 207 ÷ 9 = __________
5. 270 ÷ 6 = __________
6. 284 ÷ 4 = __________
7. 68 ÷ 2 = __________
8. 792 ÷ 8 = __________

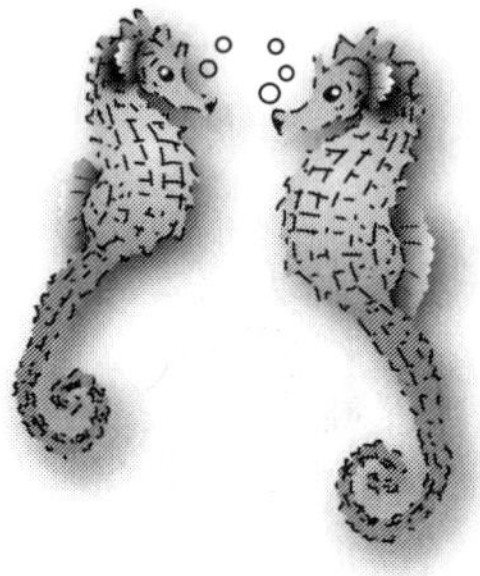

9. 234 ÷ 3 = __________
10. 140 ÷ 5 = __________
11. 301 ÷ 7 = __________
12. 198 ÷ 9 = __________
13. 148 ÷ 4 = __________
14. 126 ÷ 6 = __________
15. 136 ÷ 2 = __________
16. 496 ÷ 8 = __________

ACTIVITY 36 Twice As Nice

Name: ______________________

Date: ______________________

Divide. Some will have a remainder.

1. 178 ÷ 8 = __________
2. 370 ÷ 9 = __________
3. 454 ÷ 6 = __________
4. 107 ÷ 4 = __________
5. 112 ÷ 5 = __________
6. 303 ÷ 7 = __________
7. 162 ÷ 3 = __________
8. 97 ÷ 4 = __________

9. 729 ÷ 8 = __________
10. 178 ÷ 2 = __________
11. 111 ÷ 2 = __________
12. 218 ÷ 5 = __________
13. 235 ÷ 6 = __________
14. 443 ÷ 7 = __________
15. 113 ÷ 9 = __________
16. 59 ÷ 3 = __________

ACTIVITY 37 Twofer

Name: ______________________

Date: ______________________

Divide.

1. 192 ÷ 6 = __________
2. 485 ÷ 5 = __________
3. 42 ÷ 3 = __________
4. 91 ÷ 7 = __________
5. 120 ÷ 6 = __________
6. 440 ÷ 8 = __________
7. 160 ÷ 2 = __________
8. 228 ÷ 4 = __________

9. 430 ÷ 5 = __________
10. 376 ÷ 8 = __________
11. 225 ÷ 3 = __________
12. 468 ÷ 9 = __________
13. 630 ÷ 7 = __________
14. 150 ÷ 5 = __________
15. 360 ÷ 4 = __________
16. 352 ÷ 8 = __________

ACTIVITY 38 Twosome

Name: ______________________

Date: ______________________

Divide. Don't forget to include the remainder.

1. 117 ÷ 2 = __________
2. 235 ÷ 3 = __________
3. 94 ÷ 4 = __________
4. 137 ÷ 5 = __________
5. 483 ÷ 6 = __________
6. 379 ÷ 7 = __________
7. 555 ÷ 8 = __________
8. 228 ÷ 9 = __________

9. 323 ÷ 8 = __________
10. 214 ÷ 7 = __________
11. 529 ÷ 6 = __________
12. 212 ÷ 5 = __________
13. 62 ÷ 4 = __________
14. 194 ÷ 3 = __________
15. 161 ÷ 2 = __________
16. 183 ÷ 9 = __________

ACTIVITY 39 Race Time

Name: ____________________

Date: ____________________

Divide by 10, 20, 30, 40, or 50.

1. 950 ÷ 10 = __________
2. 900 ÷ 30 = __________
3. 900 ÷ 20 = __________
4. 440 ÷ 40 = __________
5. 430 ÷ 10 = __________
6. 350 ÷ 50 = __________
7. 550 ÷ 50 = __________
8. 180 ÷ 30 = __________
9. 160 ÷ 20 = __________
10. 360 ÷ 40 = __________
11. 500 ÷ 50 = __________
12. 640 ÷ 20 = __________
13. 330 ÷ 10 = __________
14. 210 ÷ 30 = __________
15. 480 ÷ 40 = __________
16. 150 ÷ 30 = __________

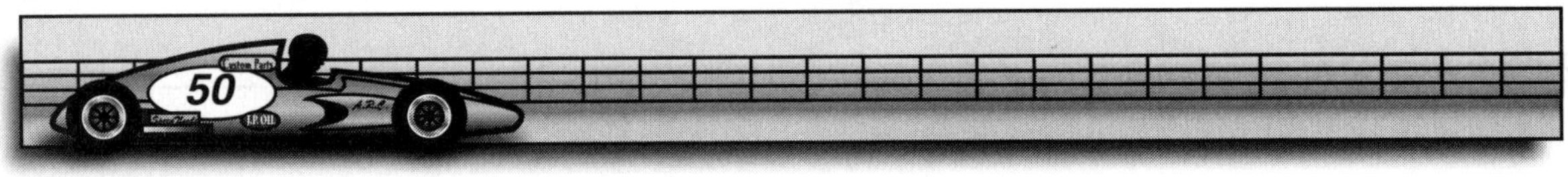

ACTIVITY 40 Speedway

Name: ____________________

Date: ____________________

Divide by 10, 20, 30, 40, or 50. Write the quotient and remainder.

1. 802 ÷ 40 = __________
2. 725 ÷ 20 = __________
3. 143 ÷ 10 = __________
4. 394 ÷ 30 = __________
5. 157 ÷ 50 = __________
6. 606 ÷ 30 = __________
7. 401 ÷ 40 = __________
8. 342 ÷ 20 = __________
9. 854 ÷ 10 = __________
10. 955 ÷ 50 = __________
11. 980 ÷ 40 = __________
12. 185 ÷ 30 = __________
13. 510 ÷ 20 = __________
14. 388 ÷ 10 = __________
15. 246 ÷ 20 = __________
16. 107 ÷ 50 = __________

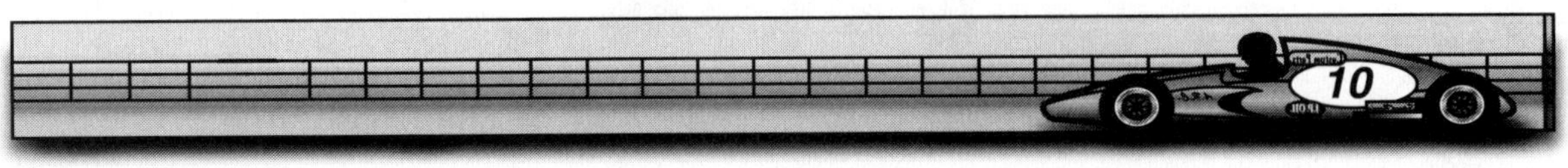

ACTIVITY 41 On Track

Name: ____________________

Date: ____________________

Divide by 50, 60, 70, 80, or 90.

1. 480 ÷ 60 = __________
2. 650 ÷ 50 = __________
3. 350 ÷ 70 = __________
4. 720 ÷ 90 = __________
5. 640 ÷ 80 = __________
6. 720 ÷ 60 = __________
7. 800 ÷ 80 = __________
8. 990 ÷ 90 = __________
9. 210 ÷ 70 = __________
10. 800 ÷ 50 = __________
11. 600 ÷ 60 = __________
12. 770 ÷ 70 = __________
13. 960 ÷ 80 = __________
14. 360 ÷ 90 = __________
15. 200 ÷ 50 = __________
16. 420 ÷ 70 = __________

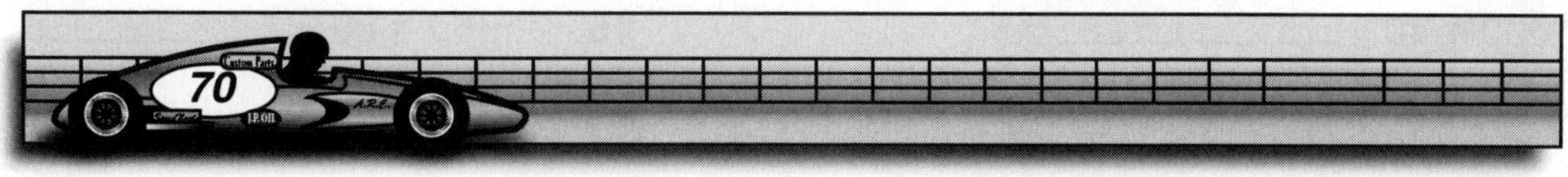

ACTIVITY 42 Qualifying Time

Name: ____________________

Date: ____________________

Divide by 50, 60, 70, 80, or 90. Write the quotient and remainder.

1. 860 ÷ 50 = __________
2. 900 ÷ 70 = __________
3. 189 ÷ 90 = __________
4. 888 ÷ 80 = __________
5. 425 ÷ 60 = __________
6. 420 ÷ 50 = __________
7. 187 ÷ 60 = __________
8. 912 ÷ 70 = __________
9. 323 ÷ 80 = __________
10. 549 ÷ 90 = __________
11. 521 ÷ 50 = __________
12. 995 ÷ 90 = __________
13. 175 ÷ 80 = __________
14. 637 ÷ 70 = __________
15. 250 ÷ 60 = __________
16. 360 ÷ 50 = __________

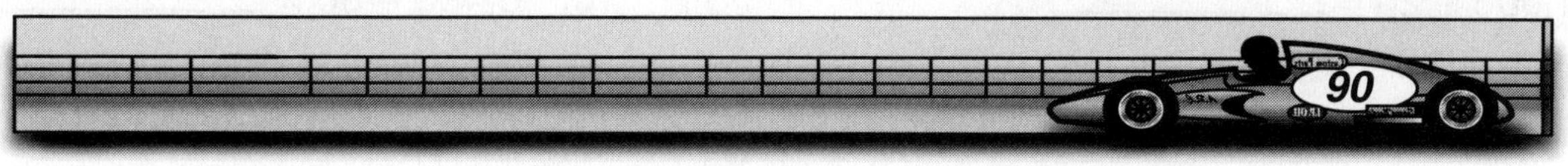

ACTIVITY 43 Start Your Engines!

Name: ____________________

Date: ____________________

Divide.

1. 7,870 ÷ 10 = __________
2. 3,990 ÷ 30 = __________
3. 1,150 ÷ 50 = __________
4. 1,050 ÷ 70 = __________
5. 1,800 ÷ 90 = __________
6. 1,840 ÷ 20 = __________
7. 1,230 ÷ 30 = __________
8. 2,000 ÷ 40 = __________

9. 4,160 ÷ 80 = __________
10. 5,410 ÷ 10 = __________
11. 6,100 ÷ 20 = __________
12. 3,480 ÷ 40 = __________
13. 1,750 ÷ 50 = __________
14. 2,190 ÷ 30 = __________
15. 1,500 ÷ 60 = __________
16. 2,960 ÷ 80 = __________

ACTIVITY 44 Green Flag

Name: ____________________

Date: ____________________

Divide. Write the quotient and remainder.

1. 2,525 ÷ 40 = __________
2. 1,037 ÷ 10 = __________
3. 3,107 ÷ 50 = __________
4. 4,870 ÷ 90 = __________
5. 3,550 ÷ 70 = __________
6. 1,355 ÷ 30 = __________
7. 2,740 ÷ 80 = __________
8. 4,008 ÷ 20 = __________

9. 4,220 ÷ 60 = __________
10. 2,245 ÷ 40 = __________
11. 6,024 ÷ 10 = __________
12. 4,640 ÷ 50 = __________
13. 2,890 ÷ 90 = __________
14. 2,807 ÷ 70 = __________
15. 1,355 ÷ 40 = __________
16. 6,488 ÷ 80 = __________

ACTIVITY 45 Rookie Driver

Name: ____________________

Date: ____________________

Divide.

1. 165 ÷ 33 = __________
2. 976 ÷ 61 = __________
3. 490 ÷ 35 = __________
4. 640 ÷ 16 = __________
5. 880 ÷ 11 = __________
6. 408 ÷ 24 = __________
7. 714 ÷ 51 = __________
8. 792 ÷ 72 = __________

9. 546 ÷ 42 = __________
10. 828 ÷ 36 = __________
11. 840 ÷ 56 = __________
12. 928 ÷ 29 = __________
13. 969 ÷ 57 = __________
14. 900 ÷ 20 = __________
15. 686 ÷ 49 = __________
16. 475 ÷ 19 = __________

ACTIVITY 46 Making Tracks

Name: ____________________

Date: ____________________

Divide. Write the quotient and remainder.

1. 495 ÷ 35 = __________
2. 499 ÷ 21 = __________
3. 239 ÷ 47 = __________
4. 970 ÷ 16 = __________
5. 656 ÷ 53 = __________
6. 190 ÷ 60 = __________
7. 715 ÷ 71 = __________
8. 544 ÷ 44 = __________
9. 808 ÷ 26 = __________
10. 466 ÷ 33 = __________
11. 309 ÷ 18 = __________
12. 475 ÷ 39 = __________
13. 638 ÷ 42 = __________
14. 855 ÷ 25 = __________
15. 110 ÷ 51 = __________
16. 135 ÷ 67 = __________

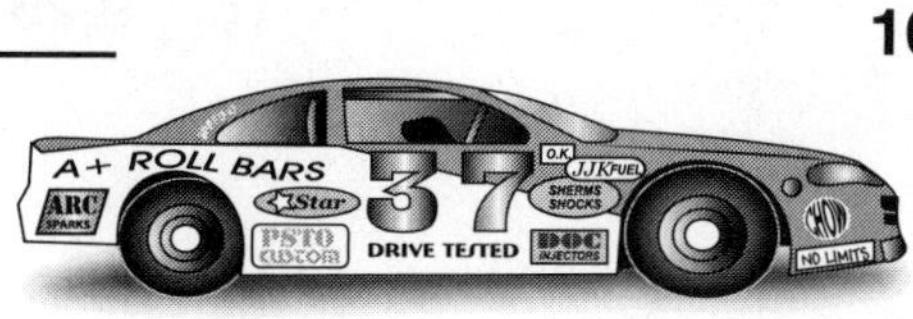

ACTIVITY 47 Race Team

Name: ______________________

Date: ______________________

Divide.

1. 1,875 ÷ 75 = __________
2. 3,395 ÷ 97 = __________
3. 5,280 ÷ 88 = __________
4. 1,575 ÷ 35 = __________
5. 5,084 ÷ 62 = __________
6. 1,484 ÷ 28 = __________
7. 2,784 ÷ 58 = __________
8. 5,356 ÷ 52 = __________

9. 6,283 ÷ 61 = __________
10. 4,920 ÷ 24 = __________
11. 5,120 ÷ 16 = __________
12. 1,617 ÷ 77 = __________
13. 1,419 ÷ 43 = __________
14. 1,827 ÷ 29 = __________
15. 1,800 ÷ 36 = __________
16. 3,564 ÷ 66 = __________

ACTIVITY 48 Pit Crew

Name: ______________________

Date: ______________________

Divide. Write the quotient and remainder.

1. 1,337 ÷ 23 = __________
2. 1,626 ÷ 45 = __________
3. 3,286 ÷ 67 = __________
4. 1,329 ÷ 83 = __________
5. 6,905 ÷ 33 = __________
6. 1,399 ÷ 15 = __________
7. 1,337 ÷ 58 = __________
8. 5,505 ÷ 55 = __________

9. 1,509 ÷ 60 = __________
10. 9,637 ÷ 47 = __________
11. 1,278 ÷ 25 = __________
12. 1,679 ÷ 39 = __________
13. 1,798 ÷ 78 = __________
14. 5,232 ÷ 13 = __________
15. 2,544 ÷ 41 = __________
16. 9,251 ÷ 74 = __________

ACTIVITY 49 Yellow Flag

Name: ____________________

Date: ____________________

Divide.

1. 68,680 ÷ 34 = ________
2. 10,563 ÷ 21 = ________
3. 27,135 ÷ 45 = ________
4. 33,344 ÷ 64 = ________
5. 23,895 ÷ 59 = ________
6. 12,426 ÷ 19 = ________
7. 29,419 ÷ 73 = ________
8. 25,200 ÷ 80 = ________

9. 29,070 ÷ 95 = ________
10. 18,226 ÷ 26 = ________
11. 16,872 ÷ 38 = ________
12. 14,700 ÷ 15 = ________
13. 22,919 ÷ 43 = ________
14. 21,728 ÷ 56 = ________
15. 67,870 ÷ 55 = ________
16. 78,540 ÷ 77 = ________

ACTIVITY 50 Driven to Succeed

Name: ____________________

Date: ____________________

Divide. Write the quotient and remainder.

1. 42,990 ÷ 90 = ________
2. 34,886 ÷ 76 = ________
3. 90,006 ÷ 36 = ________
4. 50,345 ÷ 57 = ________
5. 24,949 ÷ 44 = ________
6. 22,428 ÷ 65 = ________
7. 14,736 ÷ 29 = ________
8. 36,289 ÷ 54 = ________
9. 10,810 ÷ 24 = ________
10. 38,598 ÷ 72 = ________
11. 16,403 ÷ 33 = ________
12. 21,415 ÷ 83 = ________
13. 26,345 ÷ 37 = ________
14. 17,715 ÷ 22 = ________
15. 23,411 ÷ 52 = ________
16. 20,277 ÷ 62 = ________

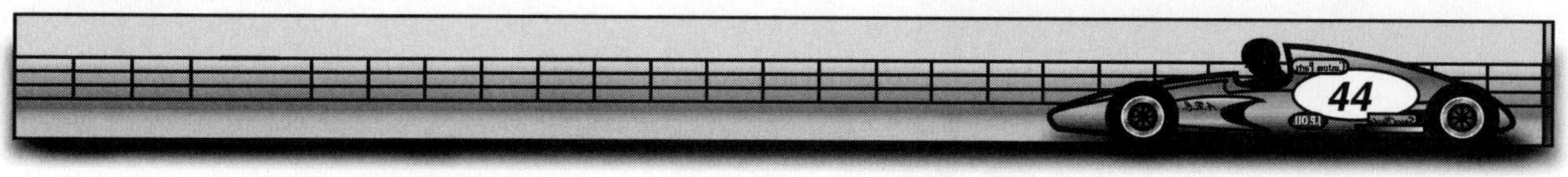

ACTIVITY 51 Checkered Flag

Name: ____________________

Date: ____________________

Divide.

1. 43,186 ÷ 26 = ____________
2. 1,134 ÷ 42 = ____________
3. 360 ÷ 72 = ____________
4. 50,524 ÷ 68 = ____________
5. 2,890 ÷ 34 = ____________
6. 960 ÷ 48 = ____________
7. 11,736 ÷ 18 = ____________
8. 1,261 ÷ 97 = ____________
9. 27,376 ÷ 58 = ____________
10. 2,700 ÷ 75 = ____________
11. 966 ÷ 69 = ____________
12. 3,444 ÷ 82 = ____________
13. 1,175 ÷ 25 = ____________
14. 3,504 ÷ 48 = ____________
15. 9,394 ÷ 77 = ____________
16. 1,887 ÷ 17 = ____________

ACTIVITY 52 Finish Line

Name: ____________________

Date: ____________________

Divide. Write the quotient and remainder.

1. 490 ÷ 32 = ____________
2. 977 ÷ 65 = ____________
3. 789 ÷ 58 = ____________
4. 853 ÷ 73 = ____________
5. 779 ÷ 45 = ____________
6. 4,231 ÷ 45 = ____________
7. 9,770 ÷ 88 = ____________
8. 4,936 ÷ 21 = ____________
9. 7,456 ÷ 35 = ____________
10. 6,477 ÷ 44 = ____________
11. 9,632 ÷ 94 = ____________
12. 60,973 ÷ 55 = ____________
13. 50,841 ÷ 37 = ____________
14. 88,442 ÷ 22 = ____________
15. 45,320 ÷ 30 = ____________
16. 65,432 ÷ 64 = ____________

ACTIVITY 53 Make a Guess

Name: ____________________

Date: ____________________

Estimate by rounding the divisor and dividend to the nearest ten or hundred. Fill in the circle of the best estimate for each quotient.

Example: 524 ÷ 11 = __?__

524 rounded to the nearest hundred = 500
11 rounded to the nearest ten = 10
500 ÷ 10 = __50__

1. 130 ÷ 24 = ____ (a.) 3 (b.) 5 (c.) 6 (d.) 50

2. 705 ÷ 47 = ____ (a.) 10 (b.) 12 (c.) 14 (d.) 20

3. 922 ÷ 61 = ____ (a.) 15 (b.) 20 (c.) 25 (d.) 30

4. 413 ÷ 35 = ____ (a.) 5 (b.) 10 (c.) 20 (d.) 25

5. 378 ÷ 52 = ____ (a.) 2 (b.) 4 (c.) 6 (d.) 8

6. 207 ÷ 18 = ____ (a.) 40 (b.) 30 (c.) 20 (d.) 10

ACTIVITY 54 A Good Guess

Name: ____________________

Date: ____________________

Estimate by rounding the divisor and dividend to the nearest ten or hundred. Fill in the circle of the best estimate for each quotient.

Example: 524 ÷ 11 = __?__

524 rounded to the nearest hundred = 500
11 rounded to the nearest ten = 10
500 ÷ 10 = __50__

1. 288 ÷ 26 = ____ (a.) 10 (b.) 20 (c.) 30 (d.) 26

2. 740 ÷ 99 = ____ (a.) 10 (b.) 7 (c.) 5 (d.) 9

3. 799 ÷ 78 = ____ (a.) 5 (b.) 80 (c.) 10 (d.) 50

4. 169 ÷ 54 = ____ (a.) 40 (b.) 4 (c.) 10 (d.) 20

5. 430 ÷ 39 = ____ (a.) 40 (b.) 10 (c.) 30 (d.) 20

6. 587 ÷ 32 = ____ (a.) 20 (b.) 32 (c.) 8 (d.) 24

ACTIVITY 55 Guesswork

Name: ____________________

Date: ____________________

Estimate by rounding the divisor to the nearest ten and the dividend to the nearest thousand. Fill in the circle of the best estimate.

1. 3,798 ÷ 43 = ______ (a.) 55 (b.) 100 (c.) 88 (d.) 60
2. 3,568 ÷ 37 = ______ (a.) 40 (b.) 90 (c.) 100 (d.) 120
3. 1,697 ÷ 77 = ______ (a.) 100 (b.) 90 (c.) 70 (d.) 25
4. 1,029 ÷ 22 = ______ (a.) 10 (b.) 150 (c.) 50 (d.) 100
5. 2,779 ÷ 62 = ______ (a.) 80 (b.) 50 (c.) 30 (d.) 100
6. 1,490 ÷ 48 = ______ (a.) 20 (b.) 50 (c.) 90 (d.) 30
7. 4,322 ÷ 21 = ______ (a.) 100 (b.) 500 (c.) 50 (d.) 200
8. 2,990 ÷ 33 = ______ (a.) 30 (b.) 60 (c.) 100 (d.) 130

ACTIVITY 56 What's Your Estimate?

Name: ____________________

Date: ____________________

Estimate by rounding the divisor to the nearest ten and the dividend to the nearest thousand. Circle the best estimate.

1. 6,321 ÷ 52 = ______ (a.) 100 (b.) 120 (c.) 150 (d.) 200
2. 5,872 ÷ 81 = ______ (a.) 75 (b.) 80 (c.) 90 (d.) 40
3. 3,908 ÷ 43 = ______ (a.) 40 (b.) 50 (c.) 70 (d.) 100
4. 2,768 ÷ 59 = ______ (a.) 35 (b.) 50 (c.) 75 (d.) 95
5. 7,540 ÷ 78 = ______ (a.) 700 (b.) 500 (c.) 300 (d.) 100
6. 4,821 ÷ 37 = ______ (a.) 125 (b.) 150 (c.) 200 (d.) 250
7. 1,758 ÷ 23 = ______ (a.) 40 (b.) 60 (c.) 80 (d.) 100
8. 2,580 ÷ 54 = ______ (a.) 10 (b.) 30 (c.) 60 (d.) 90

ACTIVITY 57 Check It Out

Name:

Date:

To check a division problem, follow these steps: Multiply the quotient by the divisor. Add the remainder. The answer will be the dividend.

Solve each problem and fill in the circle of the correct way to check it.

1. 467 ÷ 7 = ______
   - (a.) Multiply 66 by 7. Add 5.
   - (b.) Multiply 7 by 5. Add 66.
   - (c.) Add 467 and 66. Multiply by 7.

2. 832 ÷ 9 = ______
   - (a.) Multiply 92 by 9.
   - (b.) Multiply 9 by 4.
   - (c.) Multiply 92 by 9. Add 4.

3. 385 ÷ 6 = ______
   - (a.) Multiply 60 by 6. Add 4.
   - (b.) Multiply 64 by 6.
   - (c.) Multiply 64 by 6. Add 1.

4. 574 ÷ 8 = ______
   - (a.) Multiply 71 by 8. Add 6.
   - (b.) Multiply 70 by 8.
   - (c.) Multiply 69 by 8. Add 7.

ACTIVITY 58 Just Checking

Name:

Date:

To check a division problem, follow these steps: Multiply the quotient by the divisor. Add the remainder. The answer will be the dividend.

Solve each problem and fill in the circle of the correct way to check it.

1. 762 ÷ 8 = ______
   - (a.) Multiply 92 by 8. Add 5.
   - (b.) Multiply 95 by 8. Add 1.
   - (c.) Multiply 95 by 8. Add 2.

2. 489 ÷ 9 = ______
   - (a.) Multiply 50 by 9. Add 3
   - (b.) Multiply 54 by 9. Add 3.
   - (c.) Multiply 489 by 9.

3. 821 ÷ 3 = ______
   - (a.) Multiply 273 by 2. Add 3.
   - (b.) Multiply 273 by 3.
   - (c.) Multiply 273 by 3. Add 2.

4. 647 ÷ 4 = ______
   - (a.) Multiply 160 by 4. Add 6.
   - (b.) Add 647 and 3. Multiply by 4.
   - (c.) Multiply 161 by 4. Add 3.

ACTIVITY 59 Please Check

Name: ______________________

Date: ______________________

To check a division problem, follow these steps: Multiply the quotient by the divisor. Add the remainder. The answer will be the dividend.

Solve each problem and fill in the circle of the correct way to check it.

1. 432 ÷ 7 = ______
   - (a.) Multiply 7 by 5. Add 61.
   - (b.) Add 432 and 7. Multiply by 5.
   - (c.) Multiply 61 by 7. Add 5.

2. 734 ÷ 5 = ______
   - (a.) Multiply 146 by 5. Add 4.
   - (b.) Multiply 146 by 4. Add 5.
   - (c.) Add 146 and 5. Multiply by 4.

3. 528 ÷ 6 = ______
   - (a.) Multiply 528 by 6.
   - (b.) Multiply 88 by 6.
   - (c.) Add 88 and 6.

4. 375 ÷ 4 = ______
   - (a.) Multiply 90 by 4. Add 3.
   - (b.) Add 375 and 4. Multiply by 3.
   - (c.) Multiply 93 by 4. Add 3.

ACTIVITY 60 Let's Check

Name: ______________________

Date: ______________________

To check a division problem, follow these steps: Multiply the quotient by the divisor. Add the remainder. The answer will be the dividend.

Solve each problem and fill in the circle of the correct way to check it.

1. 562 ÷ 5 = ______
   - (a.) Subtract 112 from 562. Add 5.
   - (b.) Multiply 112 by 5. Add 5.
   - (c.) Multiply 112 by 5. Add 2.

2. 480 ÷ 7 = ______
   - (a.) Multiply 48 by 7.
   - (b.) Multiply 68 by 7.
   - (c.) Multiply 68 by 7. Add 4.

3. 763 ÷ 3 = ______
   - (a.) Multiply 254 by 3. Add 1.
   - (b.) Multiply 254 by 3. Add 2.
   - (c.) Multiply 254 by 3. Add 3.

4. 696 ÷ 4 = ______
   - (a.) Multiply 174 by 4.
   - (b.) Add 696 and 4. Multiply by 3.
   - (c.) Multiply 170 by 4. Add 3.

ACTIVITY 61 Helpful Hint

Name: ________________________

Date: ________________________

To divide dividends and divisors that end with zeros, use these steps:

Count the number of zeros in the divisor and cross them out.
Cross out the same number of zeros in the dividend.
Divide the numbers.
The quotient will be the same as the quotient of the original problem.

Example: 500,000 ÷ 20,000 → Cross out 4 zeros from each number.
50 ÷ 2 = 25 → so → 500,000 ÷ 20,000 = 25

Cross out the zeros and then divide.

1. 42,000 ÷ 700 = _____
2. 27,000 ÷ 3,000 = _____
3. 160,000 ÷ 800 = _____
4. 3,000,000 ÷ 5,000 = _____
5. 1,800 ÷ 90 = _____
6. 63,000,000 ÷ 900,000 = _____
7. 720,000 ÷ 80,000 = _____
8. 810,000,000 ÷ 9,000,000 = _____
9. 480,000 ÷ 60,000 = _____
10. 180 ÷ 60 = _____

ACTIVITY 62 Zero, Zip

Name: ________________________

Date: ________________________

To divide dividends and divisors that end with zeros, use these steps:

Count the number of zeros in the divisor and cross them out.
Cross out the same number of zeros in the dividend.
Divide the numbers.
The quotient will be the same as the quotient of the original problem.

Example: 500,000 ÷ 20,000 → Cross out 4 zeros from each number.
50 ÷ 2 = 25 → so → 500,000 ÷ 20,000 = 25

Cross out the zeros and then divide.

1. 88,000 ÷ 11,000 = _____
2. 700,000 ÷ 7,000 = _____
3. 36,000,000 ÷ 600,000 = _____
4. 540,000 ÷ 90,000 = _____
5. 7,700 ÷ 110 = _____
6. 550,000,000 ÷ 50,000,000 = _____
7. 42,000,000 ÷ 60,000 = _____
8. 24,000 ÷ 4,000 = _____
9. 9,600,000 ÷ 80,000 = _____
10. 3,300,000 ÷ 300,000 = _____

ACTIVITY 63 Better Than Average

Name: ______________________

Date: ______________________

To find the **average** of a group of numbers, add up the numbers and divide the answer by the number of addends.

The schedule for your basketball league has just been handed out. Find the average for each team on your roster.

Team	*Scores*				*Average Score*
Hornets	56	65	58	61	**1.**
Bobcats	47	67	64	66	**2.**
Eagles	55	48	61	60	**3.**
Shamrocks	68	59	63	66	**4.**
Spartans	58	66	60	48	**5.**

6. Which team was probably the hardest to beat?

____

ACTIVITY 64 Above Average

Name: ______________________

Date: ______________________

To find the average of a group of numbers, add up the numbers and divide the answer by the number of addends.

1. The students in Mr. Shakespeare's class earn points for each book they read.

Monday	*Tuesday*	*Wednesday*	*Thursday*	*Friday*
104	89	73	59	80

What was the average number of points the class earned a day? ____________

2. The Key Club sold fruit during lunch to earn money for their community project.

Week 1	*Week 2*	*Week 3*	*Week 4*
$208	$186	$210	$240

What was the average amount earned in a week? ____________

3. Bobby got the following grades for all the geography tests in the first quarter.

Test 1	*Test 2*	*Test 3*	*Test 4*	*Test 5*	*Test 6*
80	95	90	90	100	95

What was his average test score on his report card? ____________

ACTIVITY 65 A Good Average

Name: ____________________

Date: ____________________

To find the average of a group of numbers, add up the numbers and divide the answer by the number of addends.

Find the average of each student's math test scores.

Student	*Math Test Scores*					*Average Score*
Megan	95	98	89	94	99	**1**
Travis	90	92	94	96	98	**2.**
Chad	87	90	91	94	88	**3.**
James	98	98	99	100	100	**4.**
Martina	100	99	100	96	100	**5.**

6. Who had the highest average? ____________________

7. Who had the lowest average? ____________________

ACTIVITY 66 Average Trip

Name: ____________________

Date: ____________________

To find the average of a group of numbers, add up the numbers and divide the answer by the number of addends.

Find the average miles per trip for each florist delivery driver.

Truck 1:	21	2	13	8	**1.**
Truck 2:	2	31	16	7	**2.**
Truck 3:	11	5	3	17	**3.**
Truck 4:	25	4	4	15	**4.**
Truck 5:	15	18	21	6	**5.**

6. Which truck traveled the farthest? ____________________

ACTIVITY 67 Round It

Name: ____________________

Date: ____________________

It is important to consider the remainder when rounding. Should you round the following numbers up or down?

1. A committee is planning the Spring Fling. They need to determine the number of tables needed. Each table seats 6 people. The ticket committee sold 260 tickets.
   a. How many tables will be needed? ____________________
   b. What did you do with the remainder? Explain. ____________________
   ____

2. The Spring Fling budget has $206 for flowers. Mixed bouquets are $6.00.
   a. How many bouquets can be purchased? ____________________
   b. What did you do with the remainder? Why? ____________________
   ____

3. Each bouquet has a dozen mixed flowers.
   a. How can they be divided among the tables? ____________________
   b. What did you do with the remainder? ____________________
   ____

ACTIVITY 68 Round About

Name: ____________________

Date: ____________________

It is important to consider the remainder when rounding.
Decide whether to round the following numbers up or down if the answer must be a whole number.

1. Mason's family is moving. He is helping his mother pack the kitchen. Each box has compartments for 16 glasses. He has to pack 5 sets of glasses. Each set has 12 glasses.
   a. How many boxes will Mason need? ____________________
   b. What did you do with the remainder? Why? ____________________
   ____

2. There is $25.00 left in the budget for boxes. The boxes are $4.50 for a pack of three. The family needs 14 more boxes.
   a. How many packs will Mason buy? ____________________
   b. What did you do with the remainder? Explain. ____________________
   ____

3. Mason is packing up books. About 20 books fit in the first box. He has 87 more books to go.
   a. How many more boxes should he need? ____________________
   b. What did you do with the remainder? Explain. ____________________
   ____

ACTIVITY 69 Factor Find

Name: ____________________

Date: ____________________

To find the factors of a number, divide it by each number from 1 to itself. If the quotient has no remainder, the divisor is a factor.

Example: Find the factors of 12. →

$12 \div 1 = 12$
$12 \div 2 = 6$
$12 \div 3 = 4$
$12 \div 4 = 3$
$12 \div 6 = 2$
$12 \div 12 = 1$

→ The factors of 12 are 1, 2, 3, 4, 6, and 12.

Use division to find the factors.

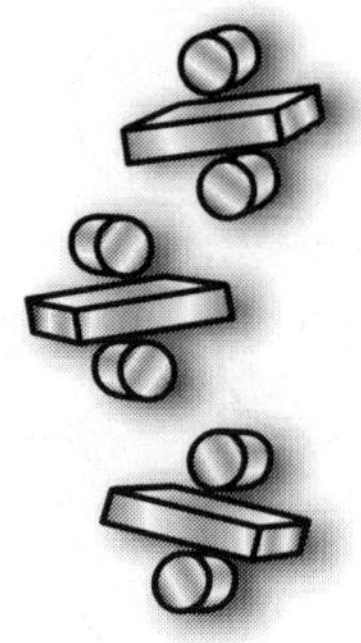

1. 20 → ____, ____, ____, ____, ____, ____
2. 18 → ____, ____, ____, ____, ____, ____
3. 70 → ____, ____, ____, ____, ____, ____, ____, ____
4. 28 → ____, ____, ____, ____, ____, ____
5. 63 → ____, ____, ____, ____, ____, ____

ACTIVITY 70 Find the GCF

Name: ____________________

Date: ____________________

Two or more numbers can have common factors, meaning factors that are the same. The greatest common factor (GCF) is the largest factor shared by both.

Example: Factors of 12: 1, 2, 3, 4, 6, 12
Factors of 42: 1, 2, 3, 6, 7, 14, 21, 42

The common factors are 1, 2, 3, and 6. The GCF is 6.

Write the greatest common factor for the set.

1. 28 70 ______
2. 15 45 ______
3. 25 100 ______
4. 18 63 ______
5. 36 48 ______
6. 19 21 ______

ACTIVITY 71 More GCF

Name: ____________________

Date: ____________________

Two or more numbers can have common factors, meaning factors that are the same. The greatest common factor (GCF) is the largest factor shared by both.

Write the greatest common factor for the set.

1. 16 40 ____
2. 24 72 ____
3. 20 32 ____
4. 49 56 ____
5. 35 70 ____
6. 30 54 ____

ACTIVITY 72 Find the GCF

Name: ____________________

Date: ____________________

Two or more numbers can have common factors, meaning factors that are the same. The greatest common factor (GCF) is the largest factor shared by all.

Write the greatest common factor for the set.

1. 24 96 44 ____
2. 18 27 30 ____
3. 50 15 25 ____
4. 30 36 66 ____
5. 45 18 54 ____
6. 22 32 88 ____

ACTIVITY 73 Find the Prime Factors

Name:____________________

Date:____________________

You know that a prime number is divisible only by itself and 1. To find the prime factors of a number, divide by prime numbers until you reach an answer of 1. (Hint: start with 2.)

Example: 18 ÷ **2** = 9
9 ÷ **3** = 3
3 ÷ **3** = 1
The prime factors of 18 are 2 x 3 x 3.

Find the prime factors for each number. List them in order from least to greatest.

1. 40 ____________________
2. 56 ____________________
3. 48 ____________________
4. 84 ____________________
5. 36 ____________________
6. 14 ____________________

ACTIVITY 74 Prime Time

Name:____________________

Date:____________________

You know that a prime number is divisible only by itself and 1. To find the prime factors of a number, divide by prime numbers until you reach an answer of 1.

Example: 81 ÷ **3** = 27
27 ÷ **3** = 9
9 ÷ **3** = 3
3 ÷ **3** = 1
Prime factors of 81 = 3 x 3 x 3 x 3

Find the prime factors for each number. List them in order from least to greatest.

1. 63 ____________________
2. 35 ____________________
3. 27 ____________________
4. 77 ____________________
5. 121 ____________________
6. 26 ____________________

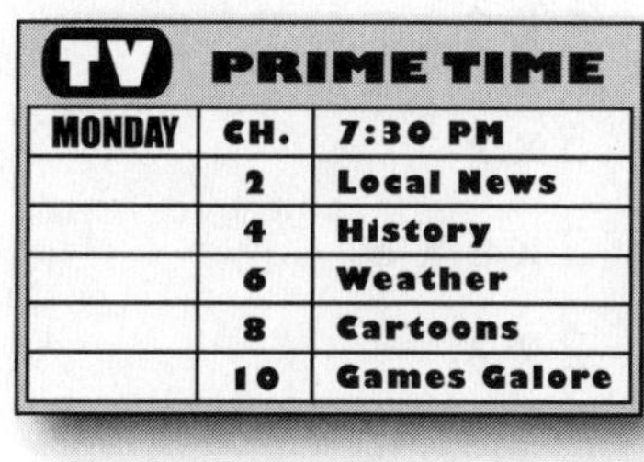

ACTIVITY 75 Find the Prime Factors

Name: ______________________

Date: ______________________

You know that a prime number is divisible only by itself and 1. To find the prime factors of a number, divide by prime numbers until you reach an answer of 1.

Example: $18 \div \mathbf{2} = 9$
$9 \div \mathbf{3} = 3$
$3 \div \mathbf{3} = 1$
The prime factors of 18 are 2 x 3 x 3.

Find the prime factors for each number. List them in order from least to greatest.

1. 52 ______________________

2. 90 ______________________

3. 33 ______________________

4. 81 ______________________

5. 72 ______________________

6. 108 ______________________

ACTIVITY 76 Prime Factorization

Name: ______________________

Date: ______________________

Fill in the circle of the correct prime factorization for each number.

1. 36
- (a.) 2 x 3 x 3
- (b.) 2 x 2 x 3
- (c.) 2 x 2 x 3 x 3
- (d.) 2 x 18

2. 84
- (a.) 2 x 3 x 7
- (b.) 2 x 2 x 3 x 7
- (c.) 2 x 3 x 7 x 21
- (d.) 2 x 3 x 3

3. 60
- (a.) 3 x 5 x 5
- (b.) 3 x 5 x 7
- (c.) 2 x 2 x 3 x 7
- (d.) 2 x 2 x 3 x 5

4. 35
- (a.) 5 x 5 x 2
- (b.) 5 x 7
- (c.) 2 x 5 x 3
- (d.) 2 x 7

5. 48
- (a.) 2 x 2 x 2 x 2 x 3
- (b.) 2 x 3 x 3 x 3
- (c.) 3 x 3 x 3
- (d.) 2 x 2 x 2 x 3

6. 16
- (a.) 2 x 7
- (b.) 2 x 2 x 3
- (c.) 2 x 2 x 2
- (d.) 2 x 2 x 2 x 2

ACTIVITY 77 Riddle Me

Name: ____________________

Date: ____________________

Can you guess the numbers?

1. It is less than 40.
It is greater than 20.
It can be divided evenly by 6.
The sum of its digits is a prime number.

My number is ____________.

2. It is less than 30.
It has two digits.
It can be divided evenly by 3.
It can be divided evenly by 7.

My number is ____________.

3. It is greater than 10.
It is less than 50.
It can be divided evenly by 9.
Divide its second digit by its first digit to get 2.

My number is ____________.

4. It is greater than 50.
It has two digits.
It can be divided evenly by 7.
The sum of its digits is 9.

My number is ____________.

ACTIVITY 78 Riddle Me

Name: ____________________

Date: ____________________

Can you guess the numbers?

1. It is less than 40.
It is greater than 20.
It can be divided evenly by 4.
The sum of its digits can be divided by 2.

My number is ____________.

2. It is greater than 40.
It is less than 60.
It can be evenly divided by 8.
Divide its second digit by its first digit to get 2.

My number is ____________.

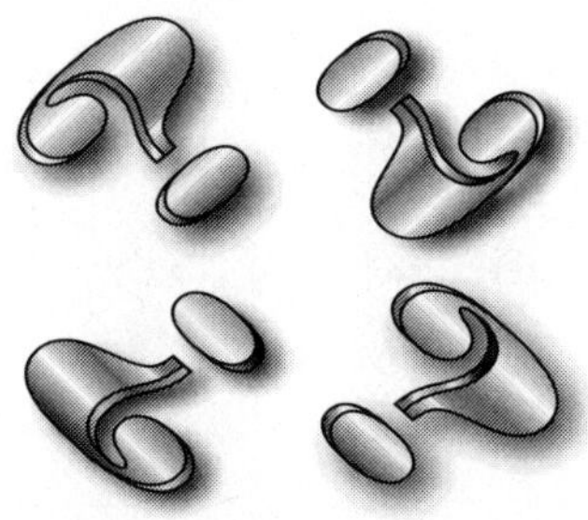

3. It is less than 20.
It has two digits.
It can be divided evenly by 5.
It can be divided evenly by 2.

My number is ____________.

4. It is greater than 50.
It has two digits.
It can be divided evenly by 11.
The sum of its digits is 14.

My number is ____________.

ACTIVITY 79 What's the Rule?

Name: ________________________

Date: ________________________

Complete the table. Write the rule that explains what is happening in the table. (Hint: Divide!)

1.

In	*Out*
15	5
18	6
21	7
24	

2.

In	*Out*
2	2
4	2
6	2
8	

ACTIVITY 80 Find the Rule

Name: ________________________

Date: ________________________

Complete the table. Write the rule that explains what is happening in the table. (Hint: Divide!)

1.

In	*Out*
60	12
55	11
50	10
40	

2.

In	*Out*
35	7
40	10
45	15
50	

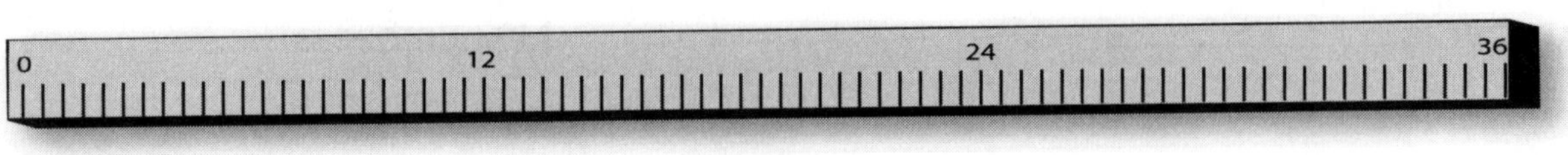

ACTIVITY 81 Chocolate Factory

Name: ______________________

Date: ______________________

Solve the word problems. Show your work.

1. Lucy works in Mrs. B's candy factory. Today she has to fill 420 boxes with chocolates. She can fill 70 boxes in an hour. If she starts at 9:00 A.M., at what time will she finish the job?

____

2. Each box of chocolates contains 2 dozen pieces. Lucy puts an equal number of chocolate cherries, chocolate nuts, and chocolate truffles in each box. How many of each kind does Lucy need to fill 70 boxes? ____

ACTIVITY 82 Chocolate Factory

Name: ______________________

Date: ______________________

Solve the word problems. Show your work.

1. Ethel drives the forklift and loads 75 cartons onto the truck every minute. A total of 1,500 boxes are loaded every minute. How many boxes are in each carton? _______________________________

2. The chocolate coating machine coats 5,000 chocolates every hour. If the machine breaks down for fifteen minutes, how many chocolates will be lost?

____

ACTIVITY 83 Bookworm

Name: ______________________

Date: ______________________

Solve the word problems. Show your work.

1. Zane loves to read during summer vacation. Last summer he read a total of 3,000 pages in 60 days. How many days did it take him to read 1,000 pages? ______________________

2. There are 15 days before school starts. Zane plans to read a Harry Potter book of 675 pages before then. How many pages will he have to read each day to finish the book by the time school starts?

____

ACTIVITY 84 Reader

Name: ______________________

Date: ______________________

Solve the word problems. Show your work.

1. Zane reads fiction and nonfiction. In fact, every third book he reads is fiction. If he reads 35 books, how many of them will be fiction? How many will be nonfiction? ______________________

____

2. Zane volunteers one hour after school five days a week at the library. He has 135 books to shelve. He can usually shelve 45 in an hour. If he starts on Tuesday, what day will he finish?

____

____

ACTIVITY 85 Hoops

Name: ____________

Date: ____________

Solve the word problems. Show your work.

1. The Comets are having a good season so far. Tonight they scored the same as they have in the last three games. The total points for all the games was 272. What did they score in each game?

____

____

2. At their home game, the Compton Comets' gym was packed. The Astros had 70 fewer fans at the game than the Comets did. If the bleachers hold 1,030 people, how many Comets fans were there? How many Astros fans? ____________

____

ACTIVITY 86 Baskets

Name: ____________

Date: ____________

Solve the word problems. Show your work.

1. Danika's team practiced for 45 minutes every day after school in the gym. In one week she made a total of 85 baskets. What was her average each day? ____________

____

2. The Astros and the Comets traveled a total of 640 miles to the state finals. The Comets traveled 26 miles further than the Astros. How far did each team travel?

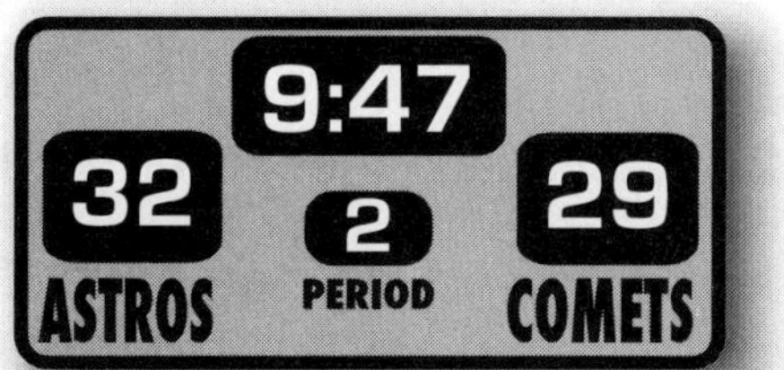

____

____

ACTIVITY 87 500 Miles

Name: ____________________

Date: ____________________

Solve the word problems. Show your work.

1. The driver of the number 6 car led 38 laps the first year he raced in the series. The next year, the number of laps led jumped to 764. In the last three years, he has led 654 laps, 393 laps, and 301 laps. How many total laps has this driver led? What is the average number of laps led by this driver per year? ____________________

____

2. In three years, the driver of the number 12 car has finished in the top ten a total of 26 times. He finished in the top ten twice in his first year. He had an equal number of top-ten finishes in each of the last two years. How many top-ten finishes did he have in those years?

____

ACTIVITY 88 Indy Racer

Name: ____________________

Date: ____________________

Solve the word problems. Show your work.

1. In 2006, a driver donated \$3 million to the Heart Center and \$2 million to the library in his hometown. In 2007, he donated \$2 million to YMCA programs and \$1 million to the Senior Center. In 2008, he gave \$4 million to divide among four other charities. On average, how much does the driver give to good causes each year? ____________________

____

2. Last year, the driver of the number 11 car had a qualifying speed of 228 miles per hour. The year before, his qualifying speed was 226 miles per hour. In the two years before that, he qualified at 216 and 230. What is his average qualifying speed? ____________________

____

ACTIVITY 89 Spelling Bee

Name: ____________________

Date: ____________________

Solve the word problems. Show your work.

1. The USA Spelling Bee has 286 contestants. There are 8 more girls entered than boys. How many girls are in the bee? How many boys? ____________________

____

2. In 2002, there were 251 spellers in the bee. In 2006, the number of spellers increased to 276. What was the actual increase between 2002 and 2006? What was the average increase per year? ____________________

____

ACTIVITY 90 Spelling Bee

Name: ____________________

Date: ____________________

Solve the word problems. Show your work.

1. The spelling bee began with 274 spellers and went for 20 rounds. No one was eliminated in the first round, but 166 were eliminated in the second. What was the average number of spellers eliminated in the remaining rounds? ____________________

____

2. The number of words used in the spelling bee has increased from 488 to 653 in the last five years. What is the average number of words added each year? If the increase continues, about how many words could there be this year? ____________________

____

ACTIVITY 91 Bead Work

Name: ____________________

Date: ____________________

Solve the word problems. Show your work.

1. Finola makes beaded necklaces in two colors—red and purple. Her red necklaces sold for 3 weeks in 2 shops. Her purple necklaces sold for 2 weeks in 5 shops. She sold 600 of each color. How many of each color sold in each shop per week? ____________________

____

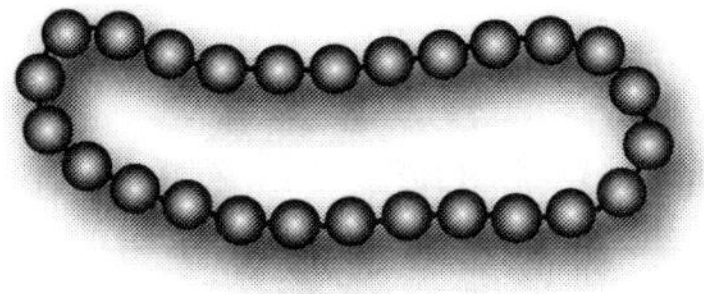

2. Finola sold bracelets at two weekend craft fairs. For the first fair, she worked 40 hours making bracelets using big beads. She sold 700 at $2.00 each. For the second fair, she worked 50 hours making bracelets with little beads. She sold 500 at $3.00 each. Which kind of bracelet should Finola make for the next fair? ____________________

____

ACTIVITY 92 Beading

Name: ____________________

Date: ____________________

Solve the word problems. Show your work.

1. Caitlin makes bead necklaces using 25 beads. She starts with 2 yellow beads. Next she places 2 green ones, and then 1 silver. How many silver beads will she need to make 20 necklaces? ____________________

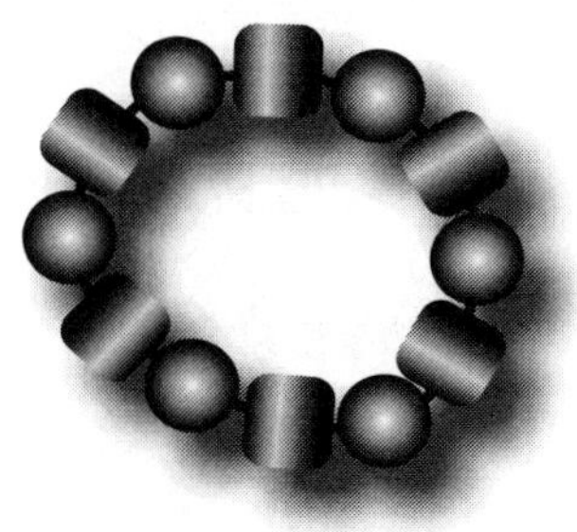

2. Caitlin bought a bag of 200 beads. She made 5 bracelets and 1 necklace. All the bracelets used the same number of beads; and the necklace had five times as many beads as one bracelet. How many beads did she use for each bracelet? ____________________

____

ACTIVITY 93 Weather Watch

Name: ______________________

Date: ______________________

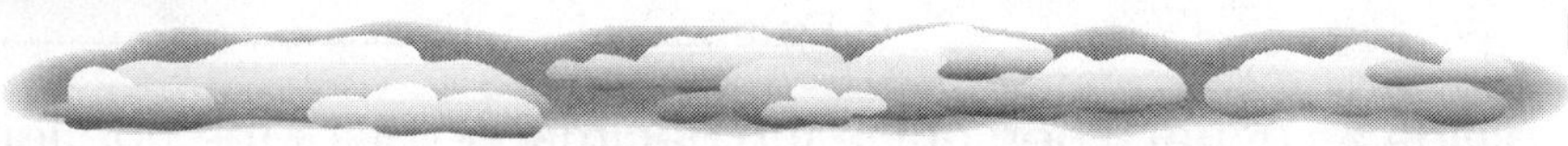

When the dividend has a decimal, divide as usual. Then place the decimal point for the quotient directly above the decimal point in the dividend.

1. $5\overline{)9.65}$
2. $4\overline{)2.92}$
3. $2\overline{)31.6}$
4. $3\overline{)18.3}$
5. $4\overline{)34.4}$
6. $8\overline{)4.64}$
7. $6\overline{)49.2}$
8. $7\overline{)20.3}$

ACTIVITY 94 Sunny Skies

Name: ______________________

Date: ______________________

When the dividend has a decimal, divide as usual. Then place the decimal point for the quotient directly above the decimal point in the dividend.

1. $3\overline{)52.2}$
2. $2\overline{)162.6}$
3. $4\overline{)229.6}$
4. $4\overline{)94.4}$

5. $7\overline{)224.7}$
6. $8\overline{)25.6}$
7. $3\overline{)35.25}$
8. $5\overline{)305.6}$

ACTIVITY 95 Summer Breeze

Name: ____________________

Date: ____________________

When the dividend has a decimal, divide as usual. Then place the decimal point for the quotient directly above the decimal point in the dividend.

1. $78\overline{)257.4}$
2. $12\overline{)30.6}$
3. $24\overline{)21.12}$
4. $41\overline{)132.02}$
5. $36\overline{)199.44}$
6. $62\overline{)942.4}$
7. $33\overline{)188.43}$
8. $59\overline{)52.51}$

ACTIVITY 96 Winter Blast

Name: ____________________

Date: ____________________

When the dividend has a decimal, divide as usual. Then place the decimal point for the quotient directly above the decimal point in the dividend.

1. $4\overline{)7.6}$
2. $7\overline{)39.9}$
3. $37\overline{)218.3}$
4. $42\overline{)432.6}$
5. $25\overline{)99.75}$
6. $9\overline{)452.25}$
7. $16\overline{)39.52}$
8. $3\overline{)255.9}$

ACTIVITY 97 Word Problems

Name: ____________________

Date: ____________________

Solve the word problems. Use your own paper if needed.

1. Benjamin bought tickets to the game for himself and his two brothers. He spent \$20.25. How much did each ticket cost? ____________________

2. Travis bought popcorn for his mom, dad, and sister at the movies. He got some for himself, too. He spent \$9.40. How much was each box of popcorn? ____________________

3. Kayla has \$15.75 to spend on 5 school lunches. How much can she spend on each school lunch? ____________________

4. Sarah bought bakery cookies for a tea party, spending \$14.34. Sarah bought 6 dozen. How much did a dozen cookies cost? ____________________

ACTIVITY 98 More Word Problems

Name: ____________________

Date: ____________________

Solve the word problems. Use your own paper if needed.

1. Claire watered Mrs. Nguyen's plants every day for a month while she was on vacation. Claire was paid \$46.40. How much did she earn per week? ____________________

2. The DeLuca family saw the Monet exhibit at the art museum. It cost \$62.50 for 5 tickets. How much was each ticket? ____________________

3. A family rented three sets of earphones for a self-guided tour at Volcano Lake for \$14.25. How much did it cost to rent a set of earphones? ____________________

4. All 26 teachers chipped in equally for a farewell gift for the night custodian. The gift cost \$109.20. How much did each person contribute? ____________________

ACTIVITY 99 Word Problems

Name: ____________________

Date: ____________________

Solve the word problems. Use your own paper if needed.

1. Faith went to the library book sale on Saturday. She purchased 10 hardcover books at $1.00 each. She also bought 23 paperbacks for $6.90. What was the price of a paperback? ____________________

2. Mr. Roberts brought sodas to the picnic. He spent $22.50 for 50 cans. How much did each can of soda cost? ____________________

3. Each box of spaghetti contains 6 one-cup servings. If Marco spends $17.50 to feed 42 people, how much does one box of spaghetti cost?

____

4. Mrs. Morgan pays $931.25 for 25 weeks of lawn care. How much does she pay per week?

____

ACTIVITY 100 More Word Problems

Name: ____________________

Date: ____________________

Solve the word problems. Use your own paper if needed.

1. Josh bought seven T-shirts to wear this summer. If he spent $69.93 on the shirts, what was the price of one shirt? ____________________

2. The lunch special at the corner deli is a bargain. If Betty buys 14 days of lunches for $60.90, how much is the special? ____________________

3. Mr. Garcia filled his pick-up truck with 30 gallons of gas. If he paid $104.70 for the gas, how much was one gallon? ____________________

4. Walker paid $75.20 for a city bus pass. He rode the bus to work and back for 32 days. How much did it cost him per day? ____________________

ACTIVITY 101 Dividing Decimals

Name: ____________________

Date: ____________________

To divide a decimal by another decimal, multiply the divisor and the dividend by a multiple of 10 to make the divisor a whole number. (You may need to add zeros to the end of the dividend as placeholders.)

Examples: $3.5\overline{)5.55}$ → multiply by 10 → $35\overline{)55.5}$

$0.02\overline{)82.2}$ → multiply by 100 → $2\overline{)8,220}$

Divide.

1. $3.8\overline{)8.36}$ **2.** $1.4\overline{)72.8}$ **3.** $2.11\overline{)13.715}$ **4.** $0.34\overline{)0.816}$

5. $0.920\overline{)3.128}$ **6.** $2.2\overline{)3.08}$ **7.** $0.77\overline{)9.24}$ **8.** $6.8\overline{)4.76}$

ACTIVITY 102 Dividing Decimals

Name: ____________________

Date: ____________________

To divide a decimal by another decimal, multiply the divisor and the dividend by a multiple of 10 to make the divisor a whole number. (You may need to add zeros to the end of the dividend as placeholders.)

Examples: $3.5\overline{)5.55}$ → multiply by 10 → $35\overline{)55.5}$

$0.02\overline{)82.2}$ → multiply by 100 → $2\overline{)8,220}$

Divide.

1. 17.94 ÷ 0.78 = ____________ **2.** 41.84 ÷ 0.08 = ____________

3. 214.4 ÷ 3.2 = ____________ **4.** 205.8 ÷ 1.4 = ____________

5. 3.48 ÷ 0.06 = ____________ **6.** 122.5 ÷ 2.5 = ____________

ACTIVITY 103 Dividing Decimals

Name: ____________________

Date: ____________________

To divide a decimal by another decimal, multiply the divisor and the dividend by a multiple of 10 to make the divisor a whole number. (You may need to add zeros to the end of the dividend as placeholders.)

Examples: $3.5\overline{)5.55}$ → multiply by 10 → $35\overline{)55.5}$

$0.02\overline{)82.2}$ → multiply by 100 → $2\overline{)8,220}$

Divide.

1. $3.2\overline{)435.2}$ **2.** $2.4\overline{)28.8}$ **3.** $1.9\overline{)68.4}$ **4.** $5.3\overline{)217.3}$

5. $0.06\overline{)3.12}$ **6.** $0.11\overline{)13.53}$ **7.** $0.7\overline{)47.60}$ **8.** $4.2\overline{)415.8}$

ACTIVITY 104 Dividing Decimals

Name: ____________________

Date: ____________________

To divide a decimal by another decimal, multiply the divisor and the dividend by a multiple of 10 to make the divisor a whole number. (You may need to add zeros to the end of the dividend as placeholders.)

Examples: $3.5\overline{)5.55}$ → multiply by 10 → $35\overline{)55.5}$

$0.02\overline{)82.2}$ → multiply by 100 → $2\overline{)8,220}$

Divide.

1. 82.5 ÷ 2.5 = ____________________ **2.** 2.52 ÷ 0.04 = ____________________

3. 11.1 ÷ 0.15 = ____________________ **4.** 22.31 ÷ 9.7 = ____________________

5. 8.32 ÷ 5.2 = ____________________ **6.** 31.11 ÷ 6.1 = ____________________

ACTIVITY 105 Reducing Fractions

Name: ____________________

Date: ____________________

To **reduce** a fraction means to find the greatest common factor and then divide.

Example: $\frac{3}{12}$ → 3: factors are 1, **3**; 12: factors are 1, 2, **3**, 4, 6, 12

The greatest common factor is 3. Divide the numerator and denominator by 3.

$\frac{3 \div 3}{12 \div 3} = \frac{1}{4}$

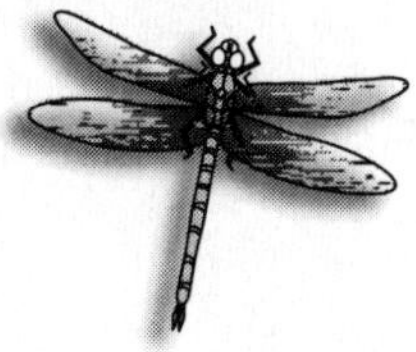

Reduce each fraction. Circle the correct answer.

1. $\frac{5}{10} =$ $\frac{1}{2}$ $\frac{10}{1}$ $\frac{1}{5}$
2. $\frac{4}{16} =$ $\frac{2}{16}$ $\frac{1}{4}$ $\frac{4}{4}$
3. $\frac{3}{24} =$ $\frac{3}{8}$ $\frac{2}{8}$ $\frac{1}{8}$
4. $\frac{12}{14} =$ $\frac{4}{6}$ $\frac{3}{5}$ $\frac{6}{7}$
5. $\frac{11}{33} =$ $\frac{1}{11}$ $\frac{1}{3}$ $\frac{1}{30}$
6. $\frac{10}{15} =$ $\frac{2}{3}$ $\frac{2}{5}$ $\frac{2}{7}$
7. $\frac{5}{25} =$ $\frac{2}{10}$ $\frac{5}{5}$ $\frac{1}{5}$
8. $\frac{3}{9} =$ $\frac{1}{6}$ $\frac{1}{3}$ $\frac{3}{3}$

ACTIVITY 106 Reducing Fractions

Name: ____________________

Date: ____________________

To **reduce** a fraction means to find the greatest common factor and then divide.

Example: $\frac{3}{12}$ → 3: factors are 1, **3**; 12: factors are 1, 2, **3**, 4, 6, 12

The greatest common factor is 3. Divide the numerator and denominator by 3.

$\frac{3 \div 3}{12 \div 3} = \frac{1}{4}$

Reduce each fraction. Circle the correct answer.

1. $\frac{4}{8} =$ $\frac{2}{3}$ $\frac{1}{2}$ $\frac{1}{4}$
2. $\frac{7}{28} =$ $\frac{7}{4}$ $\frac{1}{3}$ $\frac{1}{4}$
3. $\frac{6}{36} =$ $\frac{1}{6}$ $\frac{1}{9}$ $\frac{1}{3}$
4. $\frac{5}{10} =$ $\frac{1}{5}$ $\frac{1}{10}$ $\frac{1}{2}$
5. $\frac{11}{22} =$ $\frac{1}{11}$ $\frac{1}{5}$ $\frac{1}{2}$
6. $\frac{4}{32} =$ $\frac{1}{8}$ $\frac{1}{6}$ $\frac{1}{10}$
7. $\frac{5}{6} =$ $\frac{2}{3}$ $\frac{5}{6}$ $\frac{1}{12}$
8. $\frac{15}{24} =$ $\frac{5}{8}$ $\frac{5}{6}$ $\frac{3}{6}$

ACTIVITY 107 Reducing Fractions

Name: ____________________

Date: ____________________

To **reduce** a fraction means to find the greatest common factor and then divide.

Example: $\frac{3}{12}$ → factors are 1, **3** → factors are 1, 2, **3**, 4, 6, 12

The greatest common factor is 3. Divide the numerator and denominator by 3.

$\frac{3 \div 3}{12 \div 3} = \frac{1}{4}$

Reduce each fraction. Circle the correct answer.

1. $\frac{3}{6} =$ $\frac{1}{6}$ $\frac{2}{6}$ $\frac{1}{2}$
2. $\frac{5}{20} =$ $\frac{5}{5}$ $\frac{1}{4}$ $\frac{1}{8}$
3. $\frac{14}{28} =$ $\frac{2}{7}$ $\frac{1}{7}$ $\frac{1}{2}$
4. $\frac{3}{4} =$ $\frac{2}{3}$ $\frac{3}{4}$ $\frac{1}{8}$
5. $\frac{12}{24} =$ $\frac{6}{4}$ $\frac{1}{6}$ $\frac{1}{2}$
6. $\frac{2}{21} =$ $\frac{1}{5}$ $\frac{2}{21}$ $\frac{1}{12}$
7. $\frac{2}{16} =$ $\frac{1}{8}$ $\frac{1}{4}$ $\frac{1}{2}$
8. $\frac{3}{15} =$ $\frac{1}{3}$ $\frac{1}{5}$ $\frac{1}{15}$

ACTIVITY 108 Reducing Fractions

Name: ____________________

Date: ____________________

To **reduce** a fraction means to find the greatest common factor and then divide.

Example: $\frac{3}{12}$ → factors are 1, **3** → factors are 1, 2, **3**, 4, 6, 12

The greatest common factor is 3. Divide the numerator and denominator by 3.

$\frac{3 \div 3}{12 \div 3} = \frac{1}{4}$

Reduce each fraction. Circle the correct answer.

1. $\frac{5}{30} =$ $\frac{5}{6}$ $\frac{2}{15}$ $\frac{1}{6}$
2. $\frac{6}{18} =$ $\frac{3}{18}$ $\frac{1}{3}$ $\frac{2}{3}$
3. $\frac{4}{5} =$ $\frac{4}{5}$ $\frac{1}{5}$ $\frac{1}{4}$
4. $\frac{9}{18} =$ $\frac{1}{2}$ $\frac{1}{9}$ $\frac{1}{8}$
5. $\frac{2}{12} =$ $\frac{1}{2}$ $\frac{1}{4}$ $\frac{1}{6}$
6. $\frac{7}{32} =$ $\frac{1}{4}$ $\frac{1}{6}$ $\frac{7}{32}$
7. $\frac{8}{24} =$ $\frac{1}{3}$ $\frac{1}{4}$ $\frac{1}{5}$
8. $\frac{2}{26} =$ $\frac{1}{13}$ $\frac{2}{12}$ $\frac{2}{3}$

ACTIVITY 109 Dividing Fractions

Name: ____________________

Date: ____________________

To divide fractions: Invert the divisor (turn it upside down).
Multiply the two fractions.
Reduce to lowest terms (either divide the numerator by the denominator or divide by the greatest common factor).

Example: $\frac{2}{5} \div \frac{1}{5} = \longrightarrow \frac{2}{5} \times \frac{5}{1} = \frac{10}{5} \longrightarrow$ $10 \div 5 = 2$

Answer: $\frac{2}{5} \div \frac{1}{5} = 2$

Divide the following fractions.

1. $\frac{3}{4} \div \frac{1}{4} =$ ________ **2.** $\frac{3}{4} \div \frac{1}{3} =$ ________ **3.** $\frac{5}{12} \div \frac{6}{8} =$ ________

4. $\frac{2}{3} \div \frac{4}{6} =$ ________ **5.** $\frac{1}{8} \div \frac{2}{4} =$ ________ **6.** $\frac{2}{9} \div \frac{2}{3} =$ ________

7. $\frac{4}{5} \div \frac{1}{3} =$ ________ **8.** $\frac{4}{7} \div \frac{1}{2} =$ ________ **9.** $\frac{6}{8} \div \frac{2}{4} =$ ________

ACTIVITY 110 Dividing Fractions

Name: ____________________

Date: ____________________

To divide fractions: Invert the divisor (turn it upside down).
Multiply the two fractions.
Reduce to lowest terms (either divide the numerator by the denominator or divide by the greatest common factor).

Example: $\frac{2}{5} \div \frac{1}{5} = \longrightarrow \frac{2}{5} \times \frac{5}{1} = \frac{10}{5} \longrightarrow$ $10 \div 5 = 2$

Answer: $\frac{2}{5} \div \frac{1}{5} = 2$

Divide the following fractions.

1. $\frac{5}{9} \div \frac{2}{4} =$ ________ **2.** $\frac{2}{3} \div \frac{6}{8} =$ ________ **3.** $\frac{1}{8} \div \frac{2}{3} =$ ________

4. $\frac{5}{12} \div \frac{1}{3} =$ ________ **5.** $\frac{3}{4} \div \frac{1}{2} =$ ________ **6.** $\frac{4}{8} \div \frac{1}{4} =$ ________

7. $\frac{1}{4} \div \frac{1}{5} =$ ________ **8.** $\frac{1}{12} \div \frac{1}{5} =$ ________ **9.** $\frac{6}{7} \div \frac{1}{3} =$ ________

ACTIVITY 111 Dividing Fractions

Name: ____________________

Date: ____________________

To divide fractions: Invert the divisor (turn it upside down).
Multiply the two fractions.
Reduce to lowest terms (either divide the numerator by the denominator or divide by the greatest common factor).

Example: $\frac{2}{5} \div \frac{1}{5} = \longrightarrow \frac{2}{5} \times \frac{5}{1} = \frac{10}{5} \longrightarrow$ $10 \div 5 = 2$

Answer: $\frac{2}{5} \div \frac{1}{5} = 2$

Divide the following fractions.

1. $\frac{1}{2} \div \frac{1}{5} =$ ____________
2. $\frac{7}{16} \div \frac{4}{7} =$ ____________
3. $\frac{1}{5} \div \frac{1}{2} =$ ____________
4. $\frac{3}{4} \div \frac{3}{8} =$ ____________
5. $\frac{5}{6} \div \frac{1}{3} =$ ____________
6. $\frac{7}{9} \div \frac{1}{4} =$ ____________
7. $\frac{1}{3} \div \frac{2}{9} =$ ____________
8. $\frac{5}{9} \div \frac{1}{2} =$ ____________
9. $\frac{1}{12} \div \frac{2}{4} =$ ____________

ACTIVITY 112 Dividing Fractions

Name: ____________________

Date: ____________________

To divide fractions: Invert the divisor (turn it upside down).
Multiply the two fractions.
Reduce to lowest terms (either divide the numerator by the denominator or divide by the greatest common factor).

Example: $\frac{2}{5} \div \frac{1}{5} = \longrightarrow \frac{2}{5} \times \frac{5}{1} = \frac{10}{5} \longrightarrow$ $10 \div 5 = 2$

Answer: $\frac{2}{5} \div \frac{1}{5} = 2$

Divide the following fractions.

1. $\frac{3}{4} \div \frac{1}{9} =$ ____________
2. $\frac{7}{8} \div \frac{4}{5} =$ ____________
3. $\frac{3}{16} \div \frac{1}{10} =$ ____________
4. $\frac{1}{6} \div \frac{1}{3} =$ ____________
5. $\frac{1}{2} \div \frac{5}{8} =$ ____________
6. $\frac{2}{5} \div \frac{1}{2} =$ ____________
7. $\frac{4}{12} \div \frac{1}{2} =$ ____________
8. $\frac{1}{3} \div \frac{3}{6} =$ ____________
9. $\frac{1}{18} \div \frac{1}{3} =$ ____________

ACTIVITY 113 Dividing Fractions

Name: ____________________

Date: ____________________

To divide fractions with a common denominator, invert the divisor. The common denominators cancel, leaving you to divide the numerators.

Example: $\frac{9}{10} \div \frac{6}{10} = \rightarrow \frac{9}{\cancel{10}} \times \frac{\cancel{10}}{6} = \rightarrow \frac{9}{6} \rightarrow = 1\frac{1}{2}$

Divide the following fractions.

1. $\frac{5}{7} \div \frac{2}{7} =$ __________
2. $\frac{2}{8} \div \frac{4}{8} =$ __________
3. $\frac{8}{9} \div \frac{2}{9} =$ __________
4. $\frac{1}{3} \div \frac{2}{3} =$ __________
5. $\frac{6}{8} \div \frac{2}{8} =$ __________
6. $\frac{3}{12} \div \frac{1}{12} =$ __________
7. $\frac{4}{5} \div \frac{1}{5} =$ __________
8. $\frac{3}{4} \div \frac{5}{4} =$ __________
9. $\frac{1}{6} \div \frac{2}{6} =$ __________
10. $\frac{2}{8} \div \frac{1}{8} =$ __________
11. $\frac{5}{16} \div \frac{3}{16} =$ __________
12. $\frac{4}{12} \div \frac{2}{12} =$ __________

ACTIVITY 114 Dividing Fractions

Name: ____________________

Date: ____________________

To divide fractions with a common denominator, invert the divisor. The common denominators cancel, leaving you to divide the numerators.

Example: $\frac{9}{10} \div \frac{6}{10} = \rightarrow \frac{9}{\cancel{10}} \times \frac{\cancel{10}}{6} = \rightarrow \frac{9}{6} \rightarrow = 1\frac{1}{2}$

Divide the following fractions.

1. $\frac{3}{6} \div \frac{5}{6} =$ __________
2. $\frac{2}{9} \div \frac{4}{9} =$ __________
3. $\frac{3}{11} \div \frac{1}{11} =$ __________
4. $\frac{5}{10} \div \frac{3}{10} =$ __________
5. $\frac{3}{4} \div \frac{2}{4} =$ __________
6. $\frac{3}{8} \div \frac{2}{8} =$ __________
7. $\frac{4}{5} \div \frac{1}{5} =$ __________
8. $\frac{4}{7} \div \frac{2}{7} =$ __________
9. $\frac{2}{3} \div \frac{1}{3} =$ __________
10. $\frac{2}{7} \div \frac{3}{7} =$ __________
11. $\frac{6}{10} \div \frac{8}{10} =$ __________
12. $\frac{3}{4} \div \frac{1}{4} =$ __________

ACTIVITY 115 Dividing Fractions

Name: ____________________

Date: ____________________

Remember,
to divide fractions: Invert the divisor (turn it upside down).
Multiply the two fractions.
Reduce to lowest terms (either divide the numerator by the denominator or divide by the greatest common factor).

Example: $\frac{3}{5} \div \frac{2}{3} = \rightarrow \frac{3}{5} \times \frac{3}{2} = \rightarrow \frac{9}{10}$

Divide the following fractions.

1. $\frac{1}{3} \div \frac{3}{6} =$ ____________
2. $\frac{2}{5} \div \frac{1}{2} =$ ____________
3. $\frac{1}{6} \div \frac{1}{3} =$ ____________
4. $\frac{4}{12} \div \frac{3}{4} =$ ____________
5. $\frac{1}{2} \div \frac{5}{8} =$ ____________
6. $\frac{1}{3} \div \frac{4}{5} =$ ____________
7. $\frac{2}{5} \div \frac{1}{4} =$ ____________
8. $\frac{1}{4} \div \frac{4}{8} =$ ____________
9. $\frac{3}{4} \div \frac{1}{12} =$ ____________

ACTIVITY 116 Dividing Fractions

Name: ____________________

Date: ____________________

Remember,
to divide fractions: Invert the divisor (turn it upside down).
Multiply the two fractions.
Reduce to lowest terms (either divide the numerator by the denominator or divide by the greatest common factor).

Example: $\frac{3}{5} \div \frac{2}{3} = \rightarrow \frac{3}{5} \times \frac{3}{2} = \rightarrow \frac{9}{10}$

Divide the following fractions.

1. $\frac{3}{5} \div \frac{1}{3} =$ ____________
2. $\frac{4}{5} \div \frac{3}{15} =$ ____________
3. $\frac{3}{4} \div \frac{1}{2} =$ ____________
4. $\frac{2}{9} \div \frac{4}{18} =$ ____________
5. $\frac{3}{4} \div \frac{4}{5} =$ ____________
6. $\frac{5}{8} \div \frac{4}{5} =$ ____________
7. $\frac{5}{6} \div \frac{8}{9} =$ ____________
8. $\frac{4}{5} \div \frac{1}{3} =$ ____________
9. $\frac{3}{7} \div \frac{1}{4} =$ ____________

ACTIVITY 117 Ready for Division

Name: ____________________

Date: ____________________

Reciprocal numbers look like each other, except that one has been turned upside down. When they are multiplied, they have a product of 1.

Example: The reciprocal of $\frac{1}{4}$ is $\frac{4}{1}$.

Check: $\frac{1}{4} \times \frac{4}{1} = \frac{4}{4} = 1$

Write the reciprocal for each fraction.

1. $\frac{1}{5}$ ________ **2.** $\frac{2}{9}$ ________ **3.** $\frac{3}{4}$ ________ **4.** $\frac{2}{3}$ ________

5. $\frac{4}{6}$ ________ **6.** $\frac{3}{7}$ ________ **7.** $\frac{1}{6}$ ________ **8.** $\frac{5}{7}$ ________

9. $\frac{1}{8}$ ________ **10.** $\frac{4}{10}$ ________ **11.** $\frac{3}{5}$ ________ **12.** $\frac{4}{5}$ ________

Write the dictionary definition and a sentence.

Reciprocate: ____

____

ACTIVITY 118 Whole Numbers and Fractions

Name: ____________________

Date: ____________________

To divide a whole number by a fraction, multiply the whole number (dividend) by the reciprocal of the fraction (divisor).

Example: $2 \div \frac{3}{4} = \rightarrow \frac{2}{1} \times \frac{4}{3} = \frac{8}{3} \rightarrow 2\frac{2}{3}$

Divide using reciprocals.

1. $4 \div \frac{3}{9} =$ ________ **2.** $5 \div \frac{2}{3} =$ ________ **3.** $7 \div \frac{5}{6} =$ ________

4. $3 \div \frac{2}{6} =$ ________ **5.** $6 \div \frac{3}{4} =$ ________ **6.** $11 \div \frac{1}{6} =$ ________

7. $9 \div \frac{4}{5} =$ ________ **8.** $8 \div \frac{1}{3} =$ ________ **9.** $2 \div \frac{2}{3} =$ ________

ACTIVITY 119 Whole Numbers and Fractions

Name: ________________

Date: ________________

To divide a fraction by a whole number, multiply the fraction (dividend) by the reciprocal of the whole number (divisor).

Example: $\frac{2}{3} \div 2 = \rightarrow \frac{2}{3} \times \frac{1}{2} = \frac{2}{6} \rightarrow \frac{1}{3}$

Divide using reciprocals.

1. $\frac{2}{10} \div 5 =$ ________ **2.** $\frac{2}{4} \div 4 =$ ________ **3.** $\frac{4}{5} \div 3 =$ ________

4. $\frac{1}{5} \div 2 =$ ________ **5.** $\frac{2}{3} \div 5 =$ ________ **6.** $\frac{1}{5} \div 10 =$ ________

7. $\frac{3}{4} \div 8 =$ ________ **8.** $\frac{1}{2} \div 7 =$ ________ **9.** $\frac{1}{2} \div 2 =$ ________

ACTIVITY 120 Whole Numbers and Fractions

Name: ________________

Date: ________________

Divide using reciprocals.

1. $5 \div \frac{4}{9} =$ ________ **2.** $\frac{3}{4} \div 6 =$ ________ **3.** $8 \div \frac{6}{7} =$ ________

4. $4 \div \frac{3}{7} =$ ________ **5.** $7 \div \frac{4}{5} =$ ________ **6.** $\frac{2}{7} \div 2 =$ ________

7. $10 \div \frac{4}{5} =$ ________ **8.** $\frac{1}{3} \div 9 =$ ________ **9.** $3 \div \frac{3}{4} =$ ________

10. $\frac{2}{5} \div 9 =$ ________ **11.** $5 \div \frac{1}{7} =$ ________ **12.** $\frac{4}{5} \div 3 =$ ________

ACTIVITY 121 Dividing Mixed Numbers

Name: ______________________

Date: ______________________

To divide mixed numbers: Convert them to improper fractions.
Multiply the dividend by the reciprocal of the divisor.
Simplify the quotient.

Example: $2\frac{1}{5} \div 1\frac{1}{2} = \rightarrow \frac{11}{5} \div \frac{3}{2} = \rightarrow \frac{11}{5} \times \frac{2}{3} = \frac{22}{15} \rightarrow 1\frac{7}{15}$

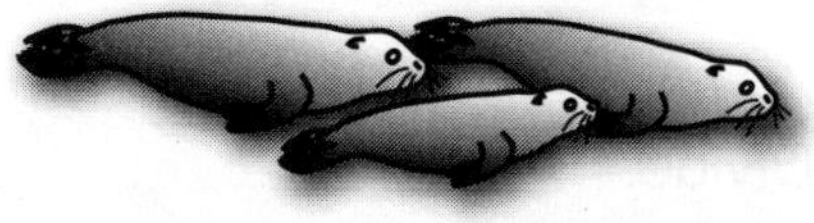

Divide.

1. $4\frac{1}{2} \div 5\frac{3}{6} =$ ________ **2.** $6\frac{1}{3} \div 2\frac{1}{2} =$ ________ **3.** $3\frac{2}{5} \div 1\frac{1}{2} =$ ________

4. $2\frac{2}{5} \div 8\frac{1}{2} =$ ________ **5.** $1\frac{3}{7} \div 2\frac{4}{5} =$ ________ **6.** $2\frac{7}{10} \div 3\frac{1}{3} =$ ________

7. $6\frac{1}{10} \div 4\frac{2}{3} =$ ________ **8.** $2\frac{7}{8} \div 4\frac{1}{4} =$ ________ **9.** $1\frac{5}{9} \div 6\frac{1}{10} =$ ________

ACTIVITY 122 Dividing Mixed Numbers

Name: ______________________

Date: ______________________

To divide mixed numbers: Convert them to improper fractions.
Multiply the dividend by the reciprocal of the divisor.
Simplify the quotient.

Example: $2\frac{1}{5} \div 1\frac{1}{2} = \rightarrow \frac{11}{5} \div \frac{3}{2} = \rightarrow \frac{11}{5} \times \frac{2}{3} = \frac{22}{15} \rightarrow 1\frac{7}{15}$

Divide.

1. $5\frac{1}{3} \div 6\frac{2}{6} =$ ________ **2.** $4\frac{1}{4} \div 5\frac{1}{2} =$ ________ **3.** $4\frac{3}{5} \div 2\frac{1}{3} =$ ________

4. $3\frac{3}{5} \div 7\frac{1}{2} =$ ________ **5.** $2\frac{1}{6} \div 2\frac{4}{5} =$ ________ **6.** $7\frac{1}{10} \div 3\frac{1}{4} =$ ________

7. $4\frac{1}{8} \div 3\frac{1}{3} =$ ________ **8.** $8\frac{4}{7} \div 4\frac{1}{4} =$ ________ **9.** $2\frac{3}{4} \div 5\frac{2}{9} =$ ________

ACTIVITY 123 Dividing Mixed Numbers

Name: ______________________

Date: ______________________

To divide mixed numbers: Convert them to improper fractions.
Multiply the dividend by the reciprocal of the divisor.
Simplify the quotient.

Example: $2\frac{1}{5} \div 1\frac{1}{2} = \rightarrow \frac{11}{5} \div \frac{3}{2} = \rightarrow \frac{11}{5} \times \frac{2}{3} = \frac{22}{15} \rightarrow 1\frac{7}{15}$

Divide.

1. $3\frac{1}{2} \div 5\frac{2}{3} =$ __________
2. $5\frac{1}{3} \div 3\frac{1}{2} =$ __________
3. $3\frac{1}{3} \div 1\frac{2}{5} =$ __________
4. $4\frac{2}{5} \div 6\frac{1}{2} =$ __________
5. $2\frac{3}{7} \div 2\frac{3}{8} =$ __________
6. $7\frac{3}{10} \div 4\frac{1}{3} =$ __________
7. $3\frac{1}{10} \div 3\frac{2}{3} =$ __________
8. $2\frac{5}{6} \div 4\frac{1}{2} =$ __________
9. $3\frac{5}{6} \div 5\frac{1}{10} =$ __________

ACTIVITY 124 Dividing Mixed Numbers

Name: ______________________

Date: ______________________

To divide mixed numbers: Convert them to improper fractions.
Multiply the dividend by the reciprocal of the divisor.
Simplify the quotient.

Example: $2\frac{1}{5} \div 1\frac{1}{2} = \rightarrow \frac{11}{5} \div \frac{3}{2} = \rightarrow \frac{11}{5} \times \frac{2}{3} = \frac{22}{15} \rightarrow 1\frac{7}{15}$

Divide.

1. $4\frac{1}{4} \div 5\frac{2}{5} =$ __________
2. $7\frac{4}{7} \div 3\frac{1}{4} =$ __________
3. $7\frac{3}{5} \div 3\frac{1}{3} =$ __________
4. $8\frac{3}{4} \div 2\frac{1}{2} =$ __________
5. $5\frac{1}{4} \div 3\frac{4}{5} =$ __________
6. $6\frac{1}{8} \div 3\frac{3}{4} =$ __________
7. $2\frac{1}{8} \div 2\frac{1}{3} =$ __________
8. $3\frac{1}{6} \div 4\frac{1}{2} =$ __________
9. $2\frac{3}{5} \div 10\frac{1}{9} =$ __________

ACTIVITY 125 Challenge

Name: ____________________

Date: ____________________

Choose the correct method of solving the division problem.

Hint: The mixed numbers are converted to improper fractions and the divisors are written as reciprocals.

1. $6\frac{1}{4} \div 3\frac{2}{5} =$ (a.) $\frac{25}{4} \times \frac{5}{17}$ (b.) $\frac{25}{4} \times \frac{17}{5}$ (c.) $\frac{4}{25} \times \frac{17}{5}$
2. $1\frac{3}{8} \div 4\frac{5}{7} =$ (a.) $\frac{8}{11} \times \frac{7}{33}$ (b.) $\frac{11}{8} \times \frac{32}{7}$ (c.) $\frac{11}{8} \times \frac{7}{33}$
3. $9\frac{3}{4} \div 3\frac{1}{5} =$ (a.) $\frac{36}{4} \times \frac{16}{5}$ (b.) $\frac{4}{39} \times \frac{16}{5}$ (c.) $\frac{39}{4} \times \frac{5}{16}$
4. $2\frac{2}{9} \div 2\frac{4}{6} =$ (a.) $\frac{20}{9} \times \frac{6}{16}$ (b.) $\frac{20}{9} \times \frac{24}{6}$ (c.) $\frac{9}{20} \times \frac{16}{6}$
5. $2\frac{1}{3} \div 3\frac{2}{5} =$ (a.) $\frac{6}{3} \times \frac{10}{5}$ (b.) $\frac{7}{3} \times \frac{5}{17}$ (c.) $\frac{3}{7} \times \frac{5}{17}$
6. $3\frac{3}{7} \div 5\frac{1}{5} =$ (a.) $\frac{24}{7} \times \frac{5}{26}$ (b.) $\frac{24}{7} \times \frac{6}{25}$ (c.) $\frac{13}{7} \times \frac{11}{5}$

ACTIVITY 126 Challenge

Name: ____________________

Date: ____________________

Choose the correct method of solving the division problem.

Hint: The mixed numbers are converted to improper fractions and the divisors are written as reciprocals.

1. $2\frac{3}{4} \div 3\frac{1}{4} =$ (a.) $\frac{13}{4} \times \frac{11}{4}$ (b.) $\frac{11}{4} \times \frac{13}{4}$ (c.) $\frac{11}{4} \times \frac{4}{13}$
2. $1\frac{3}{8} \div 2\frac{4}{7} =$ (a.) $\frac{11}{8} \times \frac{7}{18}$ (b.) $\frac{11}{8} \times \frac{7}{14}$ (c.) $\frac{12}{8} \times \frac{13}{7}$
3. $7\frac{2}{3} \div 5\frac{2}{3} =$ (a.) $\frac{72}{3} \times \frac{52}{3}$ (b.) $\frac{23}{3} \times \frac{3}{17}$ (c.) $\frac{33}{3} \times \frac{5}{17}$
4. $2\frac{3}{10} \div 2\frac{4}{12} =$ (a.) $\frac{23}{10} \times \frac{12}{28}$ (b.) $\frac{23}{10} \times \frac{28}{12}$ (c.) $\frac{15}{10} \times \frac{18}{12}$
5. $6\frac{3}{4} \div 2\frac{2}{3} =$ (a.) $\frac{13}{4} \times \frac{7}{3}$ (b.) $\frac{63}{4} \times \frac{22}{3}$ (c.) $\frac{27}{4} \times \frac{3}{8}$
6. $8\frac{1}{3} \div 2\frac{5}{6} =$ (a.) $\frac{25}{3} \times \frac{6}{17}$ (b.) $\frac{3}{25} \times \frac{17}{6}$ (c.) $\frac{25}{3} \times \frac{17}{6}$

ACTIVITY 127 More Mixed Numbers

Name: ____________________

Date: ____________________

Solve the division problems.

1. $2\frac{3}{5} \div 4\frac{1}{3} =$ ________
2. $\frac{5}{7} \div 1\frac{3}{5} =$ ________
3. $3\frac{1}{2} \div \frac{3}{5} =$ ________
4. $3\frac{1}{6} \div \frac{2}{5} =$ ________
5. $3\frac{1}{2} \div 4\frac{1}{8} =$ ________
6. $7\frac{1}{3} \div \frac{5}{9} =$ ________
7. $1\frac{3}{8} \div \frac{6}{7} =$ ________
8. $\frac{1}{3} \div 5\frac{2}{5} =$ ________
9. $3\frac{3}{7} \div \frac{1}{6} =$ ________
10. $2\frac{2}{3} \div \frac{4}{5} =$ ________
11. $6\frac{1}{4} \div 3\frac{2}{5} =$ ________
12. $7\frac{2}{3} \div 2\frac{5}{7} =$ ________

ACTIVITY 128 More Mixed Numbers

Name: ____________________

Date: ____________________

Solve the division problems.

1. $3\frac{4}{6} \div 5\frac{2}{3} =$ ________
2. $\frac{4}{7} \div 3\frac{2}{5} =$ ________
3. $7\frac{1}{2} \div \frac{2}{3} =$ ________
4. $5\frac{1}{8} \div \frac{4}{5} =$ ________
5. $1\frac{3}{4} \div 2\frac{1}{8} =$ ________
6. $6\frac{1}{3} \div \frac{3}{9} =$ ________
7. $8\frac{1}{8} \div \frac{2}{7} =$ ________
8. $\frac{2}{3} \div 3\frac{2}{7} =$ ________
9. $6\frac{3}{7} \div \frac{2}{6} =$ ________
10. $5\frac{2}{3} \div \frac{7}{8} =$ ________
11. $5\frac{1}{4} \div 2\frac{1}{5} =$ ________
12. $4\frac{2}{3} \div 1\frac{2}{5} =$ ________

ACTIVITY 129 Dividing Fractions

Name: ____________________

Date: ____________________

Solve the division problems.

1. $\frac{2}{7} \div \frac{3}{7} =$ ________
2. $\frac{4}{5} \div \frac{3}{15} =$ ________
3. $5 \div \frac{2}{3} =$ ________
4. $\frac{2}{4} \div 4 =$ ________
5. $4\frac{1}{2} \div 5\frac{1}{4} =$ ________
6. $\frac{2}{3} \div \frac{4}{6} =$ ________
7. $\frac{5}{6} \div 1\frac{2}{3} =$ ________
8. $5\frac{2}{3} \div \frac{1}{7} =$ ________
9. $\frac{5}{8} \div \frac{2}{3} =$ ________
10. $3\frac{5}{6} \div 4\frac{2}{3} =$ ________
11. $\frac{3}{4} \div \frac{2}{4} =$ ________
12. $3\frac{2}{4} \div 1\frac{4}{5} =$ ________

ACTIVITY 130 Dividing Fractions

Name: ____________________

Date: ____________________

Solve the division problems.

1. $\frac{3}{4} \div \frac{1}{2} =$ ________
2. $\frac{2}{9} \div \frac{1}{20} =$ ________
3. $4 \div \frac{5}{6} =$ ________
4. $\frac{1}{3} \div 5 =$ ________
5. $3\frac{1}{2} \div 6\frac{1}{4} =$ ________
6. $\frac{2}{5} \div \frac{1}{6} =$ ________
7. $\frac{3}{5} \div 1\frac{7}{8} =$ ________
8. $2\frac{2}{3} \div \frac{4}{7} =$ ________
9. $\frac{3}{8} \div \frac{1}{4} =$ ________
10. $5\frac{3}{4} \div 7\frac{1}{3} =$ ________
11. $\frac{1}{4} \div \frac{6}{7} =$ ________
12. $5\frac{2}{3} \div 1\frac{5}{6} =$ ________

ACTIVITY 131 Dividing Fractions

Name: ______________________

Date: ______________________

Solve the division problems.

1. $\frac{3}{5} \div \frac{1}{5} =$ __________
2. $\frac{2}{3} \div \frac{1}{3} =$ __________
3. $\frac{4}{12} \div \frac{5}{12} =$ __________
4. $\frac{1}{3} \div \frac{5}{7} =$ __________
5. $\frac{3}{4} \div \frac{6}{6} =$ __________
6. $\frac{7}{8} \div \frac{1}{6} =$ __________
7. $\frac{2}{5} \div 1\frac{5}{8} =$ __________
8. $5\frac{4}{5} \div \frac{2}{3} =$ __________
9. $\frac{1}{8} \div 5\frac{1}{4} =$ __________
10. $7\frac{1}{2} \div 7\frac{1}{4} =$ __________
11. $3\frac{2}{5} \div 5\frac{3}{7} =$ __________
12. $1\frac{2}{5} \div 2\frac{5}{6} =$ __________

ACTIVITY 132 Dividing Fractions

Name: ______________________

Date: ______________________

Solve the division problems.

1. $\frac{1}{4} \div \frac{3}{4} =$ __________
2. $\frac{2}{9} \div \frac{1}{9} =$ __________
3. $\frac{3}{6} \div \frac{5}{6} =$ __________
4. $\frac{1}{5} \div \frac{5}{6} =$ __________
5. $\frac{2}{7} \div \frac{1}{3} =$ __________
6. $\frac{3}{4} \div \frac{1}{5} =$ __________
7. $\frac{3}{5} \div 2\frac{2}{3} =$ __________
8. $5\frac{1}{4} \div \frac{3}{7} =$ __________
9. $\frac{6}{8} \div 3\frac{3}{4} =$ __________
10. $2\frac{3}{5} \div 2\frac{1}{4} =$ __________
11. $5\frac{3}{5} \div 3\frac{1}{6} =$ __________
12. $1\frac{2}{4} \div 2\frac{8}{9} =$ __________

ACTIVITY 133 Fractions to Percents

Name: ____________________

Date: ____________________

Percent means "out of 100" or "for each hundred," and is written as %. If you get a 98% on your math test, you have 98 out of 100 correct. If a fraction has a denominator of 100, it is easy to write it as a percent. Write the numerator with a % symbol.

Examples: $\frac{5}{100} = 5\%$ $\frac{25}{100} = 25\%$

Write the fractions as percents.

1. $\frac{45}{100}$ ________ 2. $\frac{50}{100}$ ________ 3. $\frac{72}{100}$ ________

4. $\frac{88}{100}$ ________ 5. $\frac{1}{100}$ ________ 6. $\frac{99}{100}$ ________

7. $\frac{100}{100}$ ________ 8. $\frac{90}{100}$ ________ 9. $\frac{35}{100}$ ________

10. $\frac{79}{100}$ ________ 11. $\frac{12}{100}$ ________ 12. $\frac{75}{100}$ ________

What does it mean when an animal hibernates 50% of the year? ____________________

____

ACTIVITY 134 Fractions to Percents

Name: ____________________

Date: ____________________

If a fraction does not have a denominator of 100, here is one way to change it to a percent.

A. Change it to a decimal by dividing the numerator by the denominator.
B. Move the decimal point two places to the right. (This is the same as multiplying by 100.)
C. Write the percent symbol.

Example: $\frac{3}{4}$ $4\overline{)3.00}$ $= \rightarrow 0.75 \rightarrow 75\%$

Change each fraction to a percent. Use the division method shown above.

1. $\frac{2}{4}$ ________ 2. $\frac{7}{10}$ ________ 3. $\frac{8}{25}$ ________

4. $\frac{3}{15}$ ________ 5. $\frac{1}{4}$ ________ 6. $\frac{2}{5}$ ________

7. $\frac{21}{50}$ ________ 8. $\frac{4}{5}$ ________ 9. $\frac{15}{20}$ ________

ACTIVITY 135 Fractions to Percents

Name: ____________________

Date: ____________________

If a fraction does not have a denominator of 100, here is one way to change it to a percent.

A. Change it to a decimal by dividing the numerator by the denominator.
B. Move the decimal point two places to the right. (This is the same as multiplying by 100.)
C. Write the percent symbol.

Example: $\frac{3}{4}$ $4\overline{)3.00}$ $= \rightarrow 0.75 \rightarrow 75\%$

Change each fraction to a percent. Use the division method shown above.

1. $\frac{1}{5}$ ________
2. $\frac{9}{10}$ ________
3. $\frac{4}{5}$ ________
4. $\frac{11}{20}$ ________
5. $\frac{18}{50}$ ________
6. $\frac{2}{4}$ ________
7. $\frac{6}{8}$ ________
8. $\frac{35}{70}$ ________
9. $\frac{18}{20}$ ________

ACTIVITY 136 Review: Fractions to Percents

Name: ____________________

Date: ____________________

Change each fraction to a percent. Use the division method.

1. $\frac{2}{10}$ ________
2. $\frac{8}{25}$ ________
3. $\frac{4}{50}$ ________
4. $\frac{12}{100}$ ________
5. $\frac{5}{20}$ ________
6. $\frac{100}{100}$ ________
7. $\frac{7}{70}$ ________
8. $\frac{25}{50}$ ________
9. $\frac{5}{25}$ ________
10. $\frac{85}{100}$ ________
11. $\frac{30}{50}$ ________
12. $\frac{250}{250}$ ________
13. $\frac{75}{75}$ ________
14. $\frac{8}{32}$ ________
15. $\frac{9}{10}$ ________

ACTIVITY 137 Finding Percents

Name: ______________________

Date: ______________________

To find a percent, divide the number you have by the number possible.

Example: Roger scored 12 out of 15 possible points on his science project. What was his percentage grade?

```
     0.80
15 ) 12.00   = 80%
     12 0
     ----
        0
```

Find the answer. Show your work on your own paper.

1. Angela spelled 20 words correctly on her spelling pretest. If there were 25 words on the test, what was her percentage score? ______________________
2. Fifty singers competed last weekend. Ten were chosen to go on to the semi-finals. What percentage of singers went to the semi-finals? ______________________
3. Alan worked 20 hours at the lake last week. What percentage of his time was the 4 hours spent cleaning the boat launch area? ______________________
4. The Friends of the Library collected 7,000 books to sell at their annual sale, including 1,750 children's books. What percentage of the total books were children's? ______________________

ACTIVITY 138 Finding Percents

Name: ______________________

Date: ______________________

To find a percent, divide the number you have by the number possible.

Example: Roger scored 12 out of 15 possible points on his science project. What was his percentage grade?

```
     0.80
15 ) 12.00   = 80%
     12 0
     ----
        0
```

Find the answer. Show your work on your own paper.

1. Fast Eddy's Car Lot sold 30 cars last weekend. The number of hybrids sold was 18. What percentage of cars sold were hybrids? ______________________
2. The lottery jackpot was up to $300 million. On Saturday at Ray's Food Store, out of 800 customers, 240 purchased lottery tickets. What percentage of customers bought tickets? ______________________
3. Of the 600 students who graduated from Eastpoint High, 90 won college scholarships. What percentage of graduates received scholarships? ______________________
4. Super Quick Delivery Service delivered 84 overnight packages and 156 second-day delivery packages. What percentage of the total packages delivered were overnight packages? ______________________

ACTIVITY 139 Mathemagical Trick: 2s

Name: ____________________

Date: ____________________

You can determine if a number is divisible by 2 without actually dividing.

Remember this rule: A number is divisible by 2 if the last digit is 0, 2, 4, 6, or 8.

Example: 2,450 is divisible by 2 because it ends in an even number.

Circle the numbers that are divisible by 2.

1.	14	28	108	33	21
2.	35	700	92	216	44
3.	1,099	4,786	7,230	566	645
4.	81	870	578	3,652	331

Choose a number you circled in row **3.** Divide by 2 and show your work.

ACTIVITY 140 Mathemagical Trick: 2s

Name: ____________________

Date: ____________________

You can determine if a number is divisible by 2 without actually dividing.

Remember this rule: A number is divisible by 2 if the last digit is 0, 2, 4, 6, or 8.

Your friends are skeptical about this math rule. Explain to them why the divisibility rule of 2 holds true. Give examples to prove your statements.

____

____

____

____

ACTIVITY 141 Mathemagical Trick: 3s

Name: ____________________

Date: ____________________

You can determine if a number is divisible by 3 without actually dividing.
Remember this rule: A number is divisible by 3 if the sum of its digits is divisible by 3.

Example: 135 = 1 + 3 + 5 = 9
9 is divisible by 3, so 135 is divisible by 3.

Circle the numbers that are divisible by 3.

1.	417	875	90	885	12
2.	980	3,483	5,415	6,001	230
3.	939	367	159	5,834	3,908
4.	35	85	344	291	6,399

Choose a number you circled in row **2.** Divide by 3 and show your work.

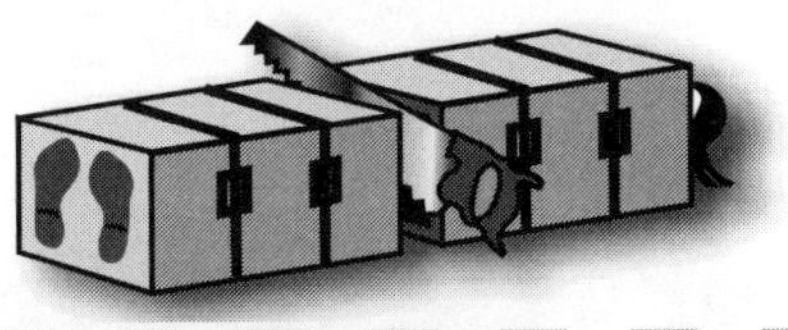

ACTIVITY 142 Mathemagical Trick: 4s

Name: ____________________

Date: ____________________

You can determine if a number is divisible by 4 without actually dividing.
Remember this rule: A number is divisible by 4 if the last two digits are divisible by 4.

Example: 544 → 44 is divisible by 4, so 544 is also divisible by 4.

Circle the numbers that are divisible by 4.

1.	748	512	16	787	660
2.	7,232	1,570	4,908	243	74
3.	581	620	64	483	8,002
4.	92	25	167	616	3,765

Choose a number you circled in Row **2.** Divide by 4 and show your work.

ACTIVITY 143 Mathemagical Trick: 4s

Name: ____________________

Date: ____________________

You can determine if a number is divisible by 4 without actually dividing.
Remember this rule: A number is divisible by 4 if the last two digits are divisible by 4.

Example: 544 → 44 is divisible by 4, so 544 is also divisible by 4.

Circle the numbers that are divisible by 4.

1.	204	872	34	548	218
2.	3,284	2,532	1,056	3,975	28
3.	416	380	53	892	5,007
4.	106	633	404	212	7,325

Choose a number you circled in Row **3.** Divide by 4 and show your work.

ACTIVITY 144 Yes or No?

Name: ____________________

Date: ____________________

Use the divisibility rules for 2, 3, and 4. Write yes or no, and explain why the number is or isn't divisible. The first one is done for you.

Number	*Divisible By*	*Yes/ No*	*Why or Why Not*
4,545	2	No	Because the last digit is not an even number.
357	3	**1.**	
88	4	**2.**	
4,892	4	**3.**	
385	3	**4.**	
2,834	2	**5.**	

ACTIVITY 145 Magical Mystery

Name: ____________________

Date: ____________________

Use the divisibility rules for 2, 3, and 4. Fill in the circle for each true statement.

1.	472	(a.) Divisible by 2	(b.) Divisible by 3	(c.) Divisible by 4
2.	5,733	(a.) Divisible by 2	(b.) Divisible by 3	(c.) Divisible by 4
3.	841	(a.) Divisible by 2	(b.) Divisible by 3	(c.) Divisible by 4
4.	2,932	(a.) Divisible by 2	(b.) Divisible by 3	(c.) Divisible by 4
5.	141	(a.) Divisible by 2	(b.) Divisible by 3	(c.) Divisible by 4
6.	54	(a.) Divisible by 2	(b.) Divisible by 3	(c.) Divisible by 4

ACTIVITY 146 Mathemagical Trick: 5s

Name: ____________________

Date: ____________________

You can determine if a number is divisible by 5 without actually dividing. Remember this rule: A number is divisible by 5 if the last digit is 0 or 5.

Example: 2,005 is divisible by 5 because the last digit is 5.

Circle the numbers that are divisible by 5.

1.	203	985	70	449	120
2.	682	4,500	7,085	3,275	440
3.	888	346	910	6,421	5,000
4.	55	73	292	599	2,705

Choose a number you circled in row **2.** Divide by 5 and show your work.

ACTIVITY 147 Mathemagical Trick: 6s

Name: ____________________

Date: ____________________

You can determine if a number is divisible by 6 without actually dividing. Remember this rule: A number is divisible by 6 if it is divisible by both 2 and 3.

Example: 138 is divisible by 2 and 3, so it is also divisible by 6.

Circle the numbers that are divisible by 6.

1.	312	30	253	488	120
2.	600	5,204	4,278	7,800	359
3.	222	63	150	3,198	5,172
4.	574	52	774	2,158	1,818

Choose a number you circled in row **4.** Divide by 6 and show your work.

ACTIVITY 148 Mathemagical Trick: 6s

Name: ____________________

Date: ____________________

You can determine if a number is divisible by 6 without actually dividing. Remember this rule: A number is divisible by 6 if it is divisible by both 2 and 3.

Example: 138 is divisible by 2 and 3, so it is also divisible by 6.

Circle the numbers that are divisible by 6.

1.	28	438	145	192	313
2.	506	4,986	3,882	2,925	738
3.	2,598	78	102	199	1,710
4.	3,123	114	342	2,654	30

Choose a number you circled in row **1.** Divide by 6 and show your work.

ACTIVITY 149 Mathemagical Trick: 7s

Name: ____________________

Date: ____________________

You can determine if a number is divisible by 7 without actually dividing.

Remember this rule: A number is divisible by 7 if you can double the last digit, subtract that number from the rest of the number, and the difference is divisible by 7.

Example: Given the number 245, double the last digit. 5 x 2 = 10
Subtract that number from 24. 24 – 10 = 14
14 is divisible by 7.
So, 245 is divisible by 7.

Circle the numbers that are divisible by 7.

1.	133	157	217	2,142	338
2.	707	3,528	375	4,277	560
3.	329	693	415	787	5,221
4.	574	175	406	379	1,571

Choose a number you circled in row **3.** Divide by 7 and show your work.

ACTIVITY 150 Mathemagical Trick: 7s

Name: ____________________

Date: ____________________

You can determine if a number is divisible by 7 without actually dividing.

Remember this rule: A number is divisible by 7 if you can double the last digit, subtract that number from the rest of the number, and the difference is divisible by 7.

Example: Given the number 245, double the last digit. 5 x 2 = 10
Subtract that number from 24. 24 – 10 = 14
14 is divisible by 7.
So, 245 is divisible by 7.

Circle the numbers that are divisible by 7.

1.	294	175	224	4,578	1,599
2.	777	651	3,644	657	245
3.	182	665	358	379	364
4.	595	308	409	469	1,488

Choose a number you circled in row **2.** Divide by 7 and show your work.

ACTIVITY 151 Yes or No?

Name: ____________________

Date: ____________________

Use the divisibility rules for 5, 6, and 7. Write yes or no, and explain why the number is or isn't evenly divisible. The first one is done for you.

Number	*Divisible By*	*Yes/ No*	*Why or Why Not*
357	7	Yes	7 x 2 = 14; 35 – 14 = 21; 21 is divisible by 7
84	6	**1.**	
8,420	5	**2.**	
224	7	**3.**	
412	6	**4.**	
355	5	**5.**	

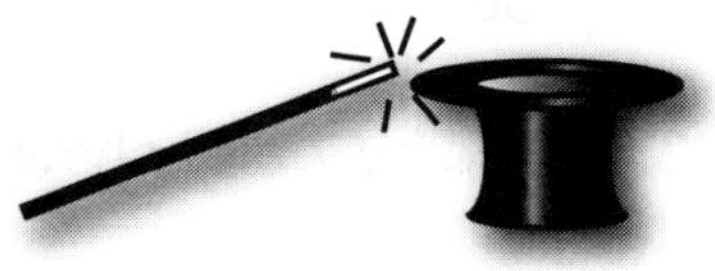

ACTIVITY 152 Magical Mystery

Name: ____________________

Date: ____________________

Use the divisibility rules for 5, 6, and 7. Fill in the circle for each true statement.

1. 150 (a.) Divisible by 5 (b.) Divisible by 6 (c.) Divisible by 7

2. 210 (a.) Divisible by 5 (b.) Divisible by 6 (c.) Divisible by 7

3. 651 (a.) Divisible by 5 (b.) Divisible by 6 (c.) Divisible by 7

4. 999 (a.) Divisible by 5 (b.) Divisible by 6 (c.) Divisible by 7

5. 85 (a.) Divisible by 5 (b.) Divisible by 6 (c.) Divisible by 7

6. 670 (a.) Divisible by 5 (b.) Divisible by 6 (c.) Divisible by 7

ACTIVITY 153 Magical Mystery

Name: ____________________

Date: ____________________

Use the divisibility rules for 5, 6, and 7. Fill in the circle for each true statement.

1. 659 — (a.) Divisible by 5 (b.) Divisible by 6 (c.) Divisible by 7
2. 540 — (a.) Divisible by 5 (b.) Divisible by 6 (c.) Divisible by 7
3. 341 — (a.) Divisible by 5 (b.) Divisible by 6 (c.) Divisible by 7
4. 777 — (a.) Divisible by 5 (b.) Divisible by 6 (c.) Divisible by 7
5. 310 — (a.) Divisible by 5 (b.) Divisible by 6 (c.) Divisible by 7
6. 1,680 — (a.) Divisible by 5 (b.) Divisible by 6 (c.) Divisible by 7

ACTIVITY 154 Mathemagical Trick: 8s

Name: ____________________

Date: ____________________

You can determine if a number is divisible by 8 without actually dividing.

Remember this rule: A number is divisible by 8 if the last three digits are divisible by 8.

Example: Is 35,120 divisible by 8?
120 is divisible by 8. $120 \div 8 = 15$
So 35,120 is divisible by 8.

Circle the numbers that are divisible by 8.

1.	1,144	5,136	4,232	7,890	2,200
2.	2,224	43,190	9,176	1,104	6,208
3.	3,136	3,478	25,208	4,160	11,458
4.	5,112	12,120	5,322	17,136	6,128

Choose a number you circled in row **3.** Divide by 8 and show your work.

ACTIVITY 155 Mathemagical Trick: 9s

Name: ____________________

Date: ____________________

You can determine if a number is divisible by 9 without actually dividing.
Remember this rule: A number is divisible by 9 if the sum of the digits is divisible by 9.

Example: Is 945 divisible by 9?
$9 + 4 + 5 = 18$
18 is divisible by 9, therefore 945 is divisible by 9.

Circle the numbers that are divisible by 9.

1.	1,224	4,131	8,802	6,190	3,220
2.	252	43,290	99,333	708	8,308
3.	7,578	569	315	891	41,319
4.	54	5,712	2,321	86	81

Choose a number you circled in row **1.** Divide by 9 and show your work.

ACTIVITY 156 Mathemagical Trick: 9s

Name: ____________________

Date: ____________________

You can determine if a number is divisible by 9 without actually dividing.
Remember this rule: A number is divisible by 9 if the sum of the digits is divisible by 9.

Example: Is 945 divisible by 9?
$9 + 4 + 5 = 18$
18 is divisible by 9, therefore 945 is divisible by 9.

Circle the numbers that are divisible by 9.

1.	108	664	712	5,301	7,305
2.	639	23,454	89,136	78	9,207
3.	68,895	72	821	395	5,367
4.	117	5,202	408	720	90

Choose a number you circled in row **3.** Divide by 9 and show your work.

ACTIVITY 157 Mathemagical Trick: 10s

Name: ____________________

Date: ____________________

You can determine if a number is divisible by 10 without actually dividing.
Remember this rule: A number is divisible by 10 if the last digit is 0.

Example: 100,450 ÷ 10 = 10,045

Circle the numbers that are divisible by 10.

1.	1,505	4,490	8,300	4,441	3,520
2.	200	5,290	99,295	401	670
3.	7,590	555	130	705,290	850,309
4.	110	5,312	6,210	95	70

Choose a number you circled in row **3.** Divide by 10 and show your work.

ACTIVITY 158 Yes or No?

Name: ____________________

Date: ____________________

Use the divisibility rules for 8, 9, and 10. Write yes or no, and explain why the number is or isn't evenly divisible. The first one is done for you.

Number	*Divisible By*	*Yes/ No*	*Why or Why Not*
995	10	No	Because it doesn't end in 0.
1,152	8	**1.**	
5,211	9	**2.**	
3,500	10	**3.**	
4,104	8	**4.**	
7,606	9	**5.**	

ACTIVITY 159 Magical Mystery

Name: ______________________

Date: ______________________

Use the divisibility rules for 8, 9, and 10. Fill in the circle for each true statement.

1. 1,120 (a.) Divisible by 8 (b.) Divisible by 9 (c.) Divisible by 10

2. 396 (a.) Divisible by 8 (b.) Divisible by 9 (c.) Divisible by 10

3. 43,780 (a.) Divisible by 8 (b.) Divisible by 9 (c.) Divisible by 10

4. 72 (a.) Divisible by 8 (b.) Divisible by 9 (c.) Divisible by 10

5. 3,240 (a.) Divisible by 8 (b.) Divisible by 9 (c.) Divisible by 10

6. 525 (a.) Divisible by 8 (b.) Divisible by 9 (c.) Divisible by 10

ACTIVITY 160 Magical Mystery

Name: ______________________

Date: ______________________

Use the divisibility rules for 8, 9, and 10. Fill in the circle for each true statement.

1. 2,160 (a.) Divisible by 8 (b.) Divisible by 9 (c.) Divisible by 10

2. 633 (a.) Divisible by 8 (b.) Divisible by 9 (c.) Divisible by 10

3. 53,210 (a.) Divisible by 8 (b.) Divisible by 9 (c.) Divisible by 10

4. 80 (a.) Divisible by 8 (b.) Divisible by 9 (c.) Divisible by 10

5. 6,144 (a.) Divisible by 8 (b.) Divisible by 9 (c.) Divisible by 10

6. 880 (a.) Divisible by 8 (b.) Divisible by 9 (c.) Divisible by 10

Answer Keys

Activity 1 (p. 3)

1. 180 ÷ 3 = 60 **2.** 60 ÷ 2 = 30
3. 30 ÷ 5 = 6 **4.** 30 ÷ 2 = 15

Activity 2 (p. 3)

1. 820; 20; 41 **2.** 3,708; 6; 618
3. 1,450; 5; 290 **4.** 400; 10; 40
5. 75; 25; 3

Activity 3 (p. 4)

1. a. 9 *r* 3 **b.** 3 *r* 2 **c.** 5 *r* 1 **d.** 30 *r* 3
2. (79) **3.** 7
4. [11] **5.** 2

Activity 4 (p. 4)

1. quotient **2.** dividend
3. remainder **4.** divisor
5. division **6.** equal
7. opposite
8. They can each have 4 slices.
9. Questions and answers will vary.

Activity 5 (p. 5)

6	6	12	18	24	30	36	42	48	54	60	66	72
5	5	10	15	20	25	30	35	40	45	50	55	60
4	4	8	12	16	20	24	28	32	36	40	44	48
3	3	6	9	12	15	18	21	24	27	30	33	36
2	2	4	6	8	10	12	14	16	18	20	22	24
1	1	2	3	4	5	6	7	8	9	10	11	12
	1	2	3	4	5	6	7	8	9	10	11	12

1. 4 **2.** 3 **3.** 10 **4.** 3
5. 3 **6.** 9 **7.** 3 **8.** 5
9. 6 **10.** 11 **11.** 6 **12.** 6
13. 11 **14.** 12 **15.** 9

Activity 6 (p. 5)

12	12	24	36	48	60	72	84	96	108	120	132	144
11	11	22	33	44	55	66	77	88	99	110	121	132
10	10	20	30	40	50	60	70	80	90	100	110	120
9	9	18	27	36	45	54	63	72	81	90	99	108
8	8	16	24	32	40	48	56	64	72	80	88	96
7	7	14	21	28	35	42	49	56	63	70	77	84
	1	2	3	4	5	6	7	8	9	10	11	12

1. 7 **2.** 9 **3.** 9 **4.** 7
5. 11 **6.** 5 **7.** 9 **8.** 11
9. 12 **10.** 11 **11.** 8 **12.** 11
13. 8 **14.** 5 **15.** 12

Activity 7 (p. 6)

1. 8, 2, 16 **2.** 6, 4, 24
3. 9, 12, 108 **4.** 5, 10, 50
5. 4, 7, 28 **6.** 3, 8, 24
7. 9, 2, 18 **8.** 10, 11, 110
9. 8, 8, 64

Activity 8 (p. 6)

1. 8, 9, 72 **2.** 7, 7, 49
3. 2, 12, 24 **4.** 12, 11, 132
5. 4, 9, 36 **6.** 9, 5, 45
7. 3, 4, 12 **8.** 8, 6, 48
9. 5, 4, 20

Activity 9 (p. 7)

2. 12 ÷ 4 = 3 or 12 ÷ 3 = 4
3. 30 ÷ 5 = 6 or 30 ÷ 6 = 5
4. 54 ÷ 6 = 9 or 54 ÷ 9 = 6
5. 14 ÷ 7 = 2 or 14 ÷ 2 = 7
6. 40 ÷ 5 = 8 or 40 ÷ 8 = 5

Activity 10 (p. 7)

2. 21 ÷ 7 = 3 or 21 ÷ 3 = 7
2. 28 ÷ 4 = 7 or 28 ÷ 7 = 4
3. 49 ÷ 7 = 7
4. 45 ÷ 5 = 9 or 45 ÷ 9 = 5
5. 32 ÷ 4 = 8 or 32 ÷ 8 = 4

Activity 11 (p. 8)

1. 5 **2.** 8 **3.** 6 **4.** 4
5. 11 **6.** 12 **7.** 7 **8.** 5
9. 9 **10.** 3 **11.** 8 **12.** 7
13. 11 **14.** 8 **15.** 8 **16.** 10

Activity 12 (p. 8)

1. 5 **2.** 2 **3.** 11 **4.** 8
5. 5 **6.** 12 **7.** 11 **8.** 4
9. 10 **10.** 8 **11.** 7 **12.** 6
13. 12 **14.** 8 **15.** 3 **16.** 12

Activity 13 (p. 9)

1. 10 *r* 1 **2.** 4 *r* 2 **3.** 7 *r* 1 **4.** 8 *r* 2
5. 9 *r* 1 **6.** 12 *r* 2 **7.** 12 *r* 1 **8.** 3 *r* 1
9. 5 *r* 3 **10.** 9 *r* 2 **11.** 7 *r* 1 **12.** 2 *r* 3
13. 5 *r* 1 **14.** 5 *r* 2 **15.** 3 *r* 1 **16.** 6 *r* 1

Activity 14 (p. 9)

1. 2 *r* 1 **2.** 7 *r* 1 **3.** 8 *r* 1 **4.** 11 *r* 2
5. 7 *r* 2 **6.** 4 *r* 2 **7.** 10 *r* 3 **8.** 3 *r* 1
9. 11 *r* 1 **10.** 5 *r* 1 **11.** 7 *r* 2 **12.** 2 *r* 2
13. 12 *r* 1 **14.** 6 *r* 1 **15.** 9 *r* 1 **16.** 9 *r* 2

Activity 15 (p. 10)
1. 6 *r* 1 **2.** 6 **3.** 2 *r* 4 **4.** 6 *r* 3
5. 5 *r* 1 **6.** 4 **7.** 10 **8.** 17 *r* 1
9. 5 *r* 2 **10.** 5 **11.** 16 *r* 1 **12.** 9 *r* 1
13. 11 **14.** 16 *r* 1 **15.** 5 *r* 3 **16.** 5 *r* 1

Activity 16 (p. 10)
1. 8 **2.** 4 *r* 4 **3.** 10 **4.** 12
5. 6 *r* 2 **6.** 8 *r* 3 **7.** 7 **8.** 10 *r* 2
9. 20 **10.** 13 *r* 4 **11.** 25 **12.** 9
13. 18 *r* 3 **14.** 22 *r* 1 **15.** 12 **16.** 21 *r* 1

Activity 17 (p. 11)
1. 52 **2.** 50 **3.** 25 **4.** 100
5. 63 **6.** 52 **7.** 49 **8.** 77
9. 120 **10.** 50 **11.** 55 **12.** 95
13. 14 **14.** 91 **15.** 142 **16.** 77

Activity 18 (p. 11)
1. b **2.** c **3.** a
4. b **5.** d **6.** a

Activity 19 (p. 12)
1. 41 *r* 1 **2.** 59 *r* 2 **3.** 50 *r* 3 **4.** 89 *r* 8
5. 80 *r* 3 **6.** 91 *r* 2 **7.** 45 *r* 5 **8.** 430 *r* 1
9. 103 *r* 1 **10.** 23 *r* 3 **11.** 31 *r* 3 **12.** 73 *r* 1
13. 61 *r* 1 **14.** 55 *r* 2 **15.** 126 *r* 2 **16.** 62 *r* 2

Activity 20 (p. 12)
1. d **2.** a **3.** c
4. c **5.** d **6.** c

Activity 21 (p. 13)
1. 78 *r* 3 **2.** 81 **3.** 90 **4.** 89 *r* 1
5. 25 **6.** 166 *r* 3 **7.** 170 *r* 1 **8.** 402
9. 19 *r* 3 **10.** 82 **11.** 57 *r* 2 **12.** 28
13. 37 *r* 1 **14.** 24 *r* 3 **15.** 49 **16.** 72

Activity 22 (p. 13)
1. 54 *r* 1 **2.** 65 *r* 1 **3.** 81 **4.** 71
5. 35 *r* 2 **6.** 51 **7.** 68 *r* 2 **8.** 23
9. 46 *r* 1 **10.** 31 *r* 1 **11.** 33 **12.** 69 *r* 2
13. 67 **14.** 39 *r* 1 **15.** 55 **16.** 88 *r* 1

Activity 23 (p. 14)
1. 339 **2.** 352 **3.** 823 **4.** 523
5. 631 **6.** 211 **7.** 737 **8.** 528
9. 1,472 **10.** 521 **11.** 685 **12.** 2,819
13. 810 **14.** 850 **15.** 723 **16.** 255

Activity 24 (p. 14)
1. 589 **2.** 532 **3.** 258 **4.** 412
5. 258 **6.** 963 **7.** 357 **8.** 357
9. 159 **10.** 1,290 **11.** 357 **12.** 654
13. 861 **14.** 698 **15.** 862 **16.** 789

Activity 25 (p. 15)
1. 682 *r* 1 **2.** 321 *r* 1 **3.** 354 *r* 2
4. 1,166 *r* 5 **5.** 352 *r* 3 **6.** 293 *r* 3
7. 546 *r* 1 **8.** 328 *r* 3 **9.** 897 *r* 1
10. 4,561 *r* 1 **11.** 591 *r* 2 **12.** 641 *r* 2
13. 359 *r* 3 **14.** 219 *r* 2 **15.** 663 *r* 2
16. 621 *r* 3

Activity 26 (p. 15)
1. d **2.** c **3.** a
4. b **5.** b **6.** d

Activity 27 (p. 16)
1. 567 *r* 1 **2.** 317 **3.** 633 *r* 2
4. 989 **5.** 634 **6.** 1,050 *r* 2
7. 503 **8.** 902 *r* 1 **9.** 450 *r* 3
10. 406 *r* 3 **11.** 830 **12.** 760 *r* 2
13. 852 *r* 1 **14.** 690 **15.** 2,109
16. 503 *r* 6

Activity 28 (p. 16)
1. 565 **2.** 805 *r* 2 **3.** 973
4. 1,153 **5.** 1,832 **6.** 852 *r* 2
7. 1,042 *r* 1 **8.** 502 *r* 1 **9.** 670
10. 270 *r* 4 **11.** 803 **12.** 328 *r* 3
13. 251 *r* 2 **14.** 328 **15.** 397 *r* 2
16. 407

Activity 29 (p. 17)
1. 7,021 **2.** 6,871 **3.** 7,852
4. 9,251 **5.** 8,231 **6.** 21,080
7. 2,007 **8.** 8,231 **9.** 3,280
10. 3,027 **11.** 7,040 **12.** 5,833
13. 3,971 **14.** 1,948 **15.** 5,210
16. 7,398

Activity 30 (p. 17)
1. 6,035 **2.** 3,400 **3.** 11,201
4. 30,070 **5.** 9,752 **6.** 8,012
7. 6,741 **8.** 7,880 **9.** 5,832
10. 2,861 **11.** 7,329 **12.** 4,088
13. 7,700 **14.** 3,870 **15.** 5,803
16. 5,493

Activity 31 (p. 18)
1. 11,172 *r* 6 **2.** 9,394 *r* 1 **3.** 21,406 *r* 1
4. 9,467 *r* 1 **5.** 7,091 *r* 4 **6.** 4,781 *r* 5
7. 15,955 *r* 1 **8.** 35,914 *r* 1 **9.** 1,643 *r* 2
10. 12,804 *r* 4 **11.** 12,642 *r* 4 **12.** 7,159 *r* 1
13. 9,265 *r* 3 **14.** 5,123 *r* 3 **15.** 13,092 *r* 1
16. 27,356 *r* 1

Activity 32 (p. 18)
1. 43,160 *r* 1 **2.** 14,195 *r* 3 **3.** 13,790 *r* 3
4. 2,938 *r* 3 **5.** 3,502 *r* 1 **6.** 4,341 *r* 1
7. 5,747 *r* 6 **8.** 4,178 *r* 6 **9.** 37,655 *r* 1
10. 13,009 *r* 1 **11.** 12,183 *r* 4 **12.** 5,662 *r* 4
13. 27,780 *r* 2 **14.** 4,635 *r* 2 **15.** 7,438 *r* 3
16. 2,283 *r* 6

Activity 33 (p. 19)
1. 11,274 *r* 2 **2.** 6,698 *r* 6 **3.** 16,142 *r* 4
4. 5,401 **5.** 47,233 **6.** 5,387
7. 2,063 *r* 1 **8.** 1,450 **9.** 5,462
10. 7,036 **11.** 12,995 *r* 2 **12.** 9,153 *r* 1
13. 22,600 **14.** 4,138 *r* 3 **15.** 2,803
16. 2,305

Activity 34 (p. 19)
1. 27,834 **2.** 2,380 **3.** 5,230 *r* 4
4. 36,991 **5.** 4,058 **6.** 15,060 *r* 4
7. 3,028 **8.** 4,963 *r* 6 **9.** 4,967 *r* 4
10. 5,228 **11.** 6,573 **12.** 3,186 *r* 1
13. 3,885 **14.** 3,473 **15.** 7,531
16. 6,322 *r* 1

Activity 35 (p. 20)
1. 55 **2.** 97 **3.** 56 **4.** 23
5. 45 **6.** 71 **7.** 34 **8.** 99
9. 78 **10.** 28 **11.** 43 **12.** 22
13. 37 **14.** 21 **15.** 68 **16.** 62

Activity 36 (p. 20)
1. 22 *r* 2 **2.** 41 *r* 1 **3.** 75 *r* 4 **4.** 26 *r* 3
5. 22 *r* 2 **6.** 43 *r* 2 **7.** 54 **8.** 24 *r* 1
9. 91 *r* 1 **10.** 89 **11.** 55 *r* 1 **12.** 43 *r* 3
13. 39 *r* 1 **14.** 63 *r* 2 **15.** 12 *r* 5 **16.** 19 *r* 2

Activity 37 (p. 21)
1. 32 **2.** 97 **3.** 14 **4.** 13
5. 20 **6.** 55 **7.** 80 **8.** 57
9. 86 **10.** 47 **11.** 75 **12.** 52
13. 90 **14.** 30 **15.** 90 **16.** 44

Activity 38 (p. 21)
1. 58 *r* 1 **2.** 78 *r* 1 **3.** 23 *r* 2 **4.** 27 *r* 2
5. 80 *r* 3 **6.** 54 *r* 1 **7.** 69 *r* 3 **8.** 25 *r* 3
9. 40 *r* 3 **10.** 30 *r* 4 **11.** 88 *r* 1 **12.** 42 *r* 2
13. 15 *r* 2 **14.** 64 *r* 2 **15.** 80 *r* 1 **16.** 20 *r* 3

Activity 39 (p. 22)
1. 95 **2.** 30 **3.** 45 **4.** 11
5. 43 **6.** 7 **7.** 11 **8.** 6
9. 8 **10.** 9 **11.** 10 **12.** 32
13. 33 **14.** 7 **15.** 12 **16.** 5

Activity 40 (p. 22)
1. 20 *r* 2 **2.** 36 *r* 5 **3.** 14 *r* 3 **4.** 13 *r* 4
5. 3 *r* 7 **6.** 20 *r* 6 **7.** 10 *r* 1 **8.** 17 *r* 2
9. 85 *r* 4 **10.** 19 *r* 5 **11.** 24 *r* 20 **12.** 6 *r* 5
13. 25 *r* 10 **14.** 38 *r* 8 **15.** 12 *r* 6 **16.** 2 *r* 7

Activity 41 (p. 23)
1. 8 **2.** 13 **3.** 5 **4.** 8
5. 8 **6.** 12 **7.** 10 **8.** 11
9. 3 **10.** 16 **11.** 10 **12.** 11
13. 12 **14.** 4 **15.** 4 **16.** 6

Activity 42 (p. 23)
1. 17 *r* 10 **2.** 12 *r* 60 **3.** 2 *r* 9 **4.** 11 *r* 8
5. 7 *r* 5 **6.** 8 *r* 20 **7.** 3 *r* 7 **8.** 13 *r* 2
9. 4 *r* 3 **10.** 6 *r* 9 **11.** 10 *r* 21 **12.** 11 *r* 5
13. 2 *r* 15 **14.** 9 *r* 7 **15.** 4 *r* 10 **16.** 7 *r* 10

Activity 43 (p. 24)
1. 787 **2.** 133 **3.** 23 **4.** 15
5. 20 **6.** 92 **7.** 41 **8.** 50
9. 52 **10.** 541 **11.** 305 **12.** 87
13. 35 **14.** 73 **15.** 25 **16.** 37

Activity 44 (p. 24)
1. 63 *r* 5 **2.** 103 *r* 7 **3.** 62 *r* 7 **4.** 54 *r* 10
5. 50 *r* 50 **6.** 45 *r* 5 **7.** 34 *r* 20 **8.** 200 *r* 8
9. 70 *r* 20 **10.** 56 *r* 5 **11.** 602 *r* 4 **12.** 92 *r* 40
13. 32 *r* 10 **14.** 40 *r* 7 **15.** 33 *r* 35 **16.** 81 *r* 8

Activity 45 (p. 25)
1. 5 **2.** 16 **3.** 14 **4.** 40
5. 80 **6.** 17 **7.** 14 **8.** 11
9. 13 **10.** 23 **11.** 15 **12.** 32
13. 17 **14.** 45 **15.** 14 **16.** 25

Activity 46 (p. 25)
1. 14 *r* 5 **2.** 23 *r* 16 **3.** 5 *r* 4 **4.** 60 *r* 10
5. 12 *r* 20 **6.** 3 *r* 10 **7.** 10 *r* 5 **8.** 12 *r* 16
9. 31 *r* 2 **10.** 14 *r* 4 **11.** 17 *r* 3 **12.** 12 *r* 7
13. 15 *r* 8 **14.** 34 *r* 5 **15.** 2 *r* 8 **16.** 2 *r* 1

Activity 47 (p. 26)
1. 25 **2.** 35 **3.** 60 **4.** 45
5. 82 **6.** 53 **7.** 48 **8.** 103
9. 103 **10.** 205 **11.** 320 **12.** 21
13. 33 **14.** 63 **15.** 50 **16.** 54

Activity 48 (p. 26)
1. 58 *r*3 **2.** 36 *r*6 **3.** 49 *r*3 **4.** 16 *r*1
5. 209 *r*8 **6.** 93 *r*4 **7.** 23 *r*3 **8.** 100 *r*5
9. 25 *r*9 **10.** 205 *r*2 **11.** 51 *r*3 **12.** 43 *r*2
13. 23 *r*4 **14.** 402 *r*6 **15.** 62 *r*2 **16.** 125 *r*1

Activity 49 (p. 27)
1. 2,020 **2.** 503 **3.** 603 **4.** 521
5. 405 **6.** 654 **7.** 403 **8.** 315
9. 306 **10.** 701 **11.** 444 **12.** 980
13. 533 **14.** 388 **15.** 1,234 **16.** 1,020

Activity 50 (p. 27)
1. 477 *r*60 **2.** 459 *r*2 **3.** 2,500 *r*6
4. 883 *r*14 **5.** 567 *r*1 **6.** 345 *r*3
7. 508 *r*4 **8.** 672 *r*1 **9.** 450 *r*10
10. 536 *r*6 **11.** 497 *r*2 **12.** 258 *r*1
13. 712 *r*1 **14.** 805 *r*5 **15.** 450 *r*11
16. 327 *r*3

Activity 51 (p. 28)
1. 1,661 **2.** 27 **3.** 5 **4.** 743
5. 85 **6.** 20 **7.** 652 **8.** 13
9. 472 **10.** 36 **11.** 14 **12.** 42
13. 47 **14.** 73 **15.** 122 **16.** 111

Activity 52 (p. 28)
1. 15 *r*10 **2.** 15 *r*2 **3.** 13 *r*35
4. 11 *r*50 **5.** 17 *r*14 **6.** 94 *r*1
7. 111 *r*2 **8.** 235 *r*1 **9.** 213 *r*1
10. 147 *r*9 **11.** 102 *r*44 **12.** 1,108 *r*33
13. 1,374 *r*3 **14.** 4,020 *r*2 **15.** 1,510 *r*20
16. 1,022 *r*24

Activity 53 (p. 29)
1. b **2.** c **3.** a
4. b **5.** d **6.** d

Activity 54 (p. 29)
1. a **2.** b **3.** c
4. b **5.** b **6.** a

Activity 55 (p. 30)
1. b **2.** c **3.** d **4.** c
5. b **6.** a **7.** d **8.** c

Activity 56 (p. 30)
1. b **2.** a **3.** d **4.** b
5. d **6.** a **7.** d **8.** c

Activity 57 (p. 31)
1. 66 *r*5; a **2.** 92 *r*4; c
3. 64 *r*1; c **4.** 71 *r*6; a

Activity 58 (p. 31)
1. 95 *r*2; c **2.** 54 *r*3; b
3. 273 *r*2; c **4.** 161 *r*3; c

Activity 59 (p. 32)
1. 61 *r*5; c **2.** 146 *r*4; a
3. 88; b **4.** 93 *r*3; c

Activity 60 (p. 32)
1. 112 *r*2; c **2.** 68 *r*4; c
3. 254 *r*1; a **4.** 174; a

Activity 61 (p. 33)
1. 6 **2.** 9 **3.** 200 **4.** 600
5. 20 **6.** 70 **7.** 9 **8.** 90
9. 8 **10.** 3

Activity 62 (p. 33)
1. 8 **2.** 100 **3.** 60 **4.** 6
5. 70 **6.** 11 **7.** 700 **8.** 6
9. 120 **10.** 11

Activity 63 (p. 34)
1. 60 **2.** 61 **3.** 56
4. 64 **5.** 58 **6.** Shamrocks

Activity 64 (p. 34)
1. 81 **2.** $211 **3.** a. 91.7

Activity 65 (p. 35)
1. 95 **2.** 94 **3.** 90
4. 99 **5.** 99 **6.** James and Martha
7. Chad

Activity 66 (p. 35)
1. 11 **2.** 14 **3.** 9
4. 12 **5.** 15 **6.** Truck 5

Activity 67 (p. 36)
1. 44 tables
   Round up, because two more seats were needed.
2. 34 bouquets
   Round down, because there wasn't enough money for more.
3. 9 flowers at each table
   Round down, because there weren't enough to add one more for each table.

Activity 68 (p. 36)

1. 4 boxes
   Round up, because he will have to pack 12 more glasses after filling 3 boxes.
2. 5 packs
   Round down, because he ran out of money, and he only needs 14 boxes.
3. 5 boxes
   Round up, because 7 extra books will need a box.

Activity 69 (p. 37)

1. 1, 2, 4, 5, 10, 20
2. 1, 2, 3, 6, 9, 18
3. 1, 2, 5, 7, 10, 14, 35, 70
4. 1, 2, 4, 7, 14, 28
5. 1, 3, 7, 9, 21, 63

Activity 70 (p. 37)

1. 14 **2.** 15 **3.** 25
4. 9 **5.** 12 **6.** 1

Activity 71 (p. 38)

1. 8 **2.** 24 **3.** 4
4. 7 **5.** 35 **6.** 6

Activity 72 (p. 38)

1. 4 **2.** 3 **3.** 5
4. 6 **5.** 9 **6.** 2

Activity 73 (p. 39)

1. 2, 2, 2, 5 **2.** 2, 2, 2, 7
3. 2, 2, 2, 2, 3 **4.** 2, 2, 3, 7
5. 2, 2, 3, 3 **6.** 2, 7

Activity 74 (p. 39)

1. 3, 3, 7 **2.** 5, 7
3. 3, 3, 3 **4.** 7, 11
5. 11, 11 **6.** 2, 13

Activity 75 (p. 40)

1. 2, 2, 13 **2.** 2, 3, 3, 5
3. 3, 11 **4.** 3, 3, 3, 3
5. 2, 2, 2, 3, 3 **6.** 2, 2, 3, 3, 3

Activity 76 (p. 40)

1. c **2.** b **3.** d
4. b **5.** a **6.** d

Activity 77 (p. 41)

1. 30 **2.** 21
3. 36 **4.** 63

Activity 78 (p. 41)

1. 28 **2.** 48
3. 10 **4.** 77

Activity 79 (p. 42)

1. 8; Divide by 3.
2. 2; Divide by 1, then by 2, then by 3, then by 4, and so on.

Activity 80 (p. 42)

1. 8; Divide by 5.
2. 25; Divide by 5, then by 4, then by 3, then by 2, and so on.

Activity 81 (p. 43)

1. 420 ÷ 70 = 6 hours; 3:00 P.M.
2. 24 ÷ 3 = 8 each; 70 x 8 = 560 candies to fill 70 boxes

Activity 82 (p. 43)

1. 1,500 ÷ 75 = 20 boxes per carton
2. 5,000 ÷ 4 = 1,250 chocolates

Activity 83 (p. 44)

1. 3,000 ÷ 60 = 50 pages per day; 1,000 ÷ 50 = 20 days
2. 675 ÷ 15 = 45 pages per day

Activity 84 (p. 44)

1. 35 ÷ 3 = 11 *r* 2; 11 fiction and 24 nonfiction
2. 135 ÷ 45 = 3 hours/days; Thursday

Activity 85 (p. 45)

1. 272 ÷ 4 = 68 points
2. 1,030 – 70 = 960; 960 ÷ 2 = 480 Astros; 480 + 70 = 550 Comets

Activity 86 (p. 45)

1. 85 ÷ 5 = 17 baskets per day
2. 640 – 26 = 614; 614 ÷ 2 = 307 Astros; 307 + 26 = 333 Comets

Activity 87 (p. 46)

1. 38 + 764 + 654 + 393 + 301 = 2,150 total laps led; 2,150 ÷ 5 years = 430 average
2. 26 – 2 = 24; 24 ÷ 2 = 12 each year

Activity 88 (p. 46)

1. 3 + 2 = \$5 million; 2 + 1 = \$3 million; \$5 + \$3 + \$4 = \$12 million; 12 ÷ 3 = \$4 million average
2. 228 + 226 + 216 + 230 = 900 ÷ 4 = 225 mph

Activity 89 (p. 47)

1. 286 – 8 = 278; 278 ÷ 2 = 139; 139 boys; 139 + 8 = 147 girls
2. 276 – 251 = 25 more actual; 25 ÷ 5 = 5 average each year

Activity 90 (p. 47)

1. 274 – 166 = 108 spellers left; 108 ÷ 18 rounds = 6 spellers in each round
2. 653 – 488 = 165 words; 165 ÷ 5 = 33 average words added each year; 653 + 33 = 686 words this year

Activity 91 (p. 48)

1. red: 600 ÷ 3 = 200; 200 ÷ 2 = 100 per week per shop
   purple: 600 ÷ 2 = 300; 300 ÷ 5 = 60 per week per shop
2. Big beads: 700 x $2 = $1,400; 1,400 ÷ 40 = $35 per hour worked
   Little beads: 500 x $3 = $1,500; 1,500 ÷ 50 = $30 per hour worked
   If she wants to make the most money in the fewest hours, she should make big-bead necklaces.

Activity 92 (p. 48)

1. 2 + 2 + 1 = 5 bead pattern; 25 ÷ 5 = 5 repeating patterns; 5 ÷ 1 = 5 silver; 20 necklaces x 5 silver = 100 silver beads
2. 5 bracelets = 1 necklace; 200 ÷ 2 = 100; 100 beads for the bracelets; 100 beads for the necklace; 100 beads ÷ 5 bracelets = 20 beads each

Activity 93 (p. 49)

1. 1.93 **2.** 0.73 **3.** 15.8
4. 6.1 **5.** 8.6 **6.** 0.58
7. 8.2 **8.** 2.9

Activity 94 (p. 49)

1. 17.4 **2.** 81.3 **3.** 57.4
4. 23.6 **5.** 32.1 **6.** 3.2
7. 11.75 **8.** 61.12

Activity 95 (p. 50)

1. 3.3 **2.** 2.55 **3.** 0.88
4. 3.22 **5.** 5.54 **6.** 15.2
7. 5.71 **8.** 0.89

Activity 96 (p. 50)

1. 1.9 **2.** 5.7 **3.** 5.9
4. 10.3 **5.** 3.99 **6.** 50.25
7. 2.47 **8.** 85.3

Activity 97 (p. 51)

1. $6.75 **2.** $2.35
3. $3.15 **4.** $2.39

Activity 98 (p. 51)

1. $11.60 **2.** $12.50
3. $4.75 **4.** $4.20

Activity 99 (p. 52)

1. $0.30 **2.** $0.45
3. $2.50 **4.** $37.25

Activity 100 (p. 52)

1. $9.99 **2.** $4.35
3. $3.49 **4.** $2.35

Activity 101 (p. 53)

1. 2.2 **2.** 52 **3.** 6.5
4. 2.4 **5.** 3.4 **6.** 1.4
7. 12 **8.** 0.7

Activity 102 (p. 53)

1. 23 **2.** 523 **3.** 67
4. 147 **5.** 58 **6.** 49

Activity 103 (p. 54)

1. 136 **2.** 12 **3.** 36 **4.** 41
5. 52 **6.** 123 **7.** 68 **8.** 99

Activity 104 (p. 54)

1. 33 **2.** 63 **3.** 74
4. 2.3 **5.** 1.6 **6.** 5.1

Activity 105 (p. 55)

1. $\frac{1}{2}$ **2.** $\frac{1}{4}$ **3.** $\frac{1}{8}$
4. $\frac{6}{7}$ **5.** $\frac{1}{3}$ **6.** $\frac{2}{3}$
7. $\frac{1}{5}$ **8.** $\frac{1}{3}$

Activity 106 (p. 55)

1. $\frac{1}{2}$ **2.** $\frac{1}{4}$ **3.** $\frac{1}{6}$
4. $\frac{1}{2}$ **5.** $\frac{1}{2}$ **6.** $\frac{1}{8}$
7. $\frac{5}{6}$ **8.** $\frac{5}{8}$

Activity 107 (p. 56)

1. $\frac{1}{2}$ **2.** $\frac{1}{4}$ **3.** $\frac{1}{2}$
4. $\frac{3}{4}$ **5.** $\frac{1}{2}$ **6.** $\frac{2}{21}$
7. $\frac{1}{8}$ **8.** $\frac{1}{5}$

Activity 108 (p. 56)

1. $\frac{1}{6}$ **2.** $\frac{1}{3}$ **3.** $\frac{4}{5}$
4. $\frac{1}{2}$ **5.** $\frac{1}{6}$ **6.** $\frac{7}{32}$
7. $\frac{1}{3}$ **8.** $\frac{1}{13}$

Activity 109 (p. 57)

1. 3 **2.** $2\frac{1}{4}$ **3.** $\frac{5}{9}$
4. 1 **5.** $\frac{1}{4}$ **6.** $\frac{1}{3}$
7. $2\frac{2}{5}$ **8.** $1\frac{1}{7}$ **9.** $1\frac{1}{2}$

Activity 110 (p. 57)

1. $1\frac{1}{9}$ **2.** $\frac{8}{9}$ **3.** $\frac{3}{16}$
4. $1\frac{1}{4}$ **5.** $1\frac{1}{2}$ **6.** 2
7. $1\frac{1}{4}$ **8.** $\frac{5}{12}$ **9.** $2\frac{4}{7}$

Activity 111 (p. 58)

1. $2\frac{1}{2}$ **2.** $\frac{49}{64}$ **3.** $\frac{2}{5}$
4. 2 **5.** $2\frac{1}{2}$ **6.** $3\frac{1}{9}$
7. $1\frac{1}{2}$ **8.** $1\frac{1}{9}$ **9.** $\frac{1}{6}$

Activity 112 (p. 58)

1. $6\frac{3}{4}$ **2.** $1\frac{3}{32}$ **3.** $1\frac{7}{8}$
4. $\frac{1}{2}$ **5.** $\frac{4}{5}$ **6.** $\frac{4}{5}$
7. $\frac{2}{3}$ **8.** $\frac{2}{3}$ **9.** $\frac{1}{6}$

Activity 113 (p. 59)

1. $2\frac{1}{2}$ **2.** $\frac{1}{2}$ **3.** 4
4. $\frac{1}{2}$ **5.** 3 **6.** 3
7. 4 **8.** $\frac{3}{5}$ **9.** $\frac{1}{2}$
10. 2 **11.** $1\frac{2}{3}$ **12.** 2

Activitiy 114 (p. 59)

1. $\frac{3}{5}$ **2.** $\frac{1}{2}$ **3.** 3
4. $1\frac{2}{3}$ **5.** $1\frac{1}{2}$ **6.** 1
7. 4 **8.** 2 **9.** 2
10. $\frac{2}{3}$ **11.** $\frac{3}{4}$ **12.** 3

Activity 115 (p. 60)

1. $\frac{2}{3}$ **2.** $\frac{4}{5}$ **3.** $\frac{1}{2}$
4. $\frac{4}{9}$ **5.** $\frac{4}{5}$ **6.** $\frac{5}{12}$
7. $1\frac{3}{5}$ **8.** $\frac{1}{2}$ **9.** 9

Activity 116 (p. 60)

1. $1\frac{4}{5}$ **2.** 4 **3.** $1\frac{1}{2}$
4. 1 **5.** $\frac{15}{16}$ **6.** $\frac{25}{32}$
7. $\frac{15}{16}$ **8.** $2\frac{2}{5}$ **9.** $1\frac{5}{7}$

Activity 117 (p. 61)

1. $\frac{5}{1}$ **2.** $\frac{9}{2}$ **3.** $\frac{4}{3}$ **4.** $\frac{3}{2}$
5. $\frac{6}{4}$ **6.** $\frac{7}{3}$ **7.** $\frac{6}{1}$ **8.** $\frac{7}{5}$
9. $\frac{8}{1}$ **10.** $\frac{10}{4}$ **11.** $\frac{5}{3}$ **12.** $\frac{5}{4}$

Reciprocate: to give and take mutually; to return in kind or degree
Sentences will vary.

Activity 118 (p. 61)

1. 12 **2.** $7\frac{1}{2}$ **3.** $8\frac{2}{5}$
4. 9 **5.** 8 **6.** 66
7. $11\frac{1}{4}$ **8.** 24 **9.** 3

Activity 119 (p. 62)

1. $\frac{1}{25}$ **2.** $\frac{1}{8}$ **3.** $\frac{4}{15}$
4. $\frac{1}{10}$ **5.** $\frac{2}{15}$ **6.** $\frac{1}{50}$
7. $\frac{3}{32}$ **8.** $\frac{1}{14}$ **9.** $\frac{1}{4}$

Activity 120 (p. 62)

1. $11\frac{1}{4}$ **2.** $\frac{1}{8}$ **3.** $9\frac{1}{3}$
4. $9\frac{1}{3}$ **5.** $8\frac{3}{4}$ **6.** $\frac{1}{7}$
7. $12\frac{1}{2}$ **8.** $\frac{1}{27}$ **9.** 4
10. $\frac{2}{45}$ **11.** 35 **12.** $\frac{4}{15}$

Activity 121 (p. 63)

1. $\frac{9}{11}$ **2.** $2\frac{8}{15}$ **3.** $2\frac{4}{15}$
4. $\frac{24}{85}$ **5.** $\frac{25}{49}$ **6.** $\frac{81}{100}$
7. $1\frac{43}{140}$ **8.** $\frac{23}{34}$ **9.** $\frac{140}{549}$

Activity 122 (p. 63)

1. $\frac{16}{19}$ **2.** $\frac{17}{22}$ **3.** $1\frac{34}{35}$
4. $\frac{12}{25}$ **5.** $\frac{65}{84}$ **6.** $2\frac{12}{65}$
7. $1\frac{19}{80}$ **8.** $2\frac{2}{119}$ **9.** $\frac{99}{188}$

Activity 123 (p. 64)

1. $\frac{21}{34}$ **2.** $1\frac{11}{21}$ **3.** $2\frac{8}{21}$
4. $\frac{44}{65}$ **5.** $1\frac{3}{133}$ **6.** $1\frac{89}{130}$
7. $\frac{93}{110}$ **8.** $\frac{17}{27}$ **9.** $\frac{115}{153}$

Activity 124 (p. 64)
1. $\frac{85}{108}$ **2.** $2\frac{30}{91}$ **3.** $2\frac{7}{25}$
4. $3\frac{1}{2}$ **5.** $1\frac{29}{76}$ **6.** $1\frac{19}{30}$
7 $\frac{51}{56}$ **8.** $\frac{19}{27}$ **9.** $\frac{9}{35}$

Activity 125 (p. 65)
1. a **2.** c **3.** c
4. a **5.** b **6.** a

Activity 126 (p. 65)
1. c **2.** a **3.** b
4. a **5.** c **6.** a

Activity 127 (p. 66)
1. $\frac{3}{5}$ **2.** $\frac{25}{56}$ **3.** $5\frac{5}{6}$
4. $7\frac{11}{12}$ **5.** $\frac{28}{33}$ **6.** $13\frac{1}{5}$
7. $1\frac{29}{48}$ **8.** $\frac{5}{81}$ **9.** $20\frac{4}{7}$
10. $3\frac{1}{3}$ **11.** $1\frac{57}{68}$ **12.** $2\frac{47}{57}$

Activity 128 (p. 66)
1. $1\frac{5}{17}$ **2.** $\frac{20}{119}$ **3.** $11\frac{1}{4}$
4. $6\frac{13}{32}$ **5.** $\frac{14}{17}$ **6.** 19
7. $28\frac{7}{16}$ **8.** $\frac{14}{69}$ **9.** $19\frac{2}{7}$
10. $6\frac{10}{21}$ **11.** $2\frac{17}{44}$ **12.** $3\frac{1}{3}$

Activity 129 (p. 67)
1. $\frac{2}{3}$ **2.** 4 **3.** $7\frac{1}{2}$
4. $\frac{1}{8}$ **5.** $\frac{6}{7}$ **6.** 1
7. $\frac{1}{2}$ **8.** $39\frac{2}{3}$ **9.** $\frac{15}{16}$
10. $\frac{23}{28}$ **11.** $1\frac{1}{2}$ **12.** $1\frac{17}{18}$

Activity 130 (p. 67)
1. $1\frac{1}{2}$ **2.** $4\frac{4}{9}$ **3.** $4\frac{4}{5}$
4. $\frac{1}{15}$ **5.** $\frac{14}{25}$ **6.** $2\frac{2}{5}$
7. $\frac{8}{25}$ **8.** $4\frac{2}{3}$ **9.** $1\frac{1}{2}$
10. $\frac{69}{88}$ **11.** $\frac{7}{24}$ **12.** $3\frac{1}{11}$

Activity 131 (p. 68)
1. 3 **2.** 2 **3.** $\frac{4}{5}$
4. $\frac{7}{15}$ **5.** $\frac{3}{4}$ **6.** $5\frac{1}{4}$
7. $\frac{16}{65}$ **8.** $8\frac{7}{10}$ **9.** $\frac{1}{42}$
10. $1\frac{1}{29}$ **11.** $\frac{119}{190}$ **12.** $\frac{42}{85}$

Activity 132 (p. 68)
1. $\frac{1}{3}$ **2.** 2 **3.** $\frac{3}{5}$
4. $\frac{6}{25}$ **5.** $\frac{6}{7}$ **6.** $3\frac{3}{4}$
7. $\frac{9}{40}$ **8.** $12\frac{1}{4}$ **9.** $\frac{1}{5}$
10. $1\frac{7}{45}$ **11.** $1\frac{73}{95}$ **12.** $\frac{27}{52}$

Activity 133 (p. 69)
1. 45% **2.** 50% **3.** 72%
4. 88% **5.** 1% **6.** 99%
7. 100% **8.** 90% **9.** 35%
10. 79% **11.** 12% **12.** 75%
It sleeps one-half of the year.

Activity 134 (p. 69)
1. 50% **2.** 70% **3.** 32%
4. 20% **5.** 25% **6.** 40%
7. 42% **8.** 80% **9.** 75%

Activity 135 (p. 70)
1. 20% **2.** 90% **3.** 80%
4. 55% **5.** 36% **6.** 50%
7. 75% **8.** 50% **9.** 90%

Activity 136 (p. 70)
1. 20% **2.** 32% **3.** 8%
4. 12% **5.** 25% **6.** 100%
7. 10% **8.** 50% **9.** 20%
10. 85% **11.** 60% **12.** 100%
13. 100% **14.** 25% **15.** 90%

Activity 137 (p. 71)
1. 80% **2.** 20%
3. 20% **4.** 25%

Activity 138 (p. 71)
1. 60% **2.** 30%
3. 15% **4.** 35%

Activity 139 (p. 72)
1. 14; 28; 108
2. 700; 92; 216; 44
3. 4,786; 7,230; 566
4. 870; 578; 3,652
Answers will vary.

Activity 140 (p. 72)
Answers will vary.

Activity 141 (p. 73)
1. 417; 90; 885; 12
2. 3,483; 5,415;
3. 939; 159
4. 291; 6,399
Answers will vary.

Activity 142 (p. 73)
1. 748; 512; 16; 660
2. 7,232; 4,908
3. 620; 64
4. 92; 616
Answers will vary.

Activity 143 (p. 74)
1. 204; 872; 548
2. 3,284; 2,532; 1,056; 28
3. 416; 380; 892
4. 404; 212
Answers will vary.

Activity 144 (p. 74)
1. Yes Sum of digits (15) is divisible by 3
2. Yes Last two digits (88) divisible by 4
3. Yes Last two digits (92) divisible by 4
4. No Sum of digits (16) is not divisible by 3
5. Yes Last digit (4) is an even number

Activity 145 (p. 75)
1. a, c **2.** b **3.** none
4. a, c **5.** b **6.** a, b

Activity 146 (p. 75)
1. 985; 70; 120
2. 4,500; 7,085; 3,275; 440
3. 910; 5,000
4. 55; 2,705
Answers will vary.

Activity 147 (p. 76)
1. 312; 30; 120
2. 600; 4,278; 7,800
3. 222; 150; 3,198; 5,172
4. 774; 1,818
Answers will vary.

Activity 148 (p. 76)
1. 438; 192
2. 4,986; 3,882; 738
3. 2,598; 78; 102; 1,710
4. 114; 342; 30
Answers will vary.

Activity 149 (p. 77)
1. 133; 217; 2,142
2. 707; 3,528; 4,277; 560
3. 329; 693
4. 574; 175; 406
Answers will vary.

Activity 150 (p. 77)
1. 294; 175; 224; 4,578
2. 777; 651; 245
3. 182; 665; 364
4. 595; 308; 469
Answers will vary.

Activity 151 (p. 78)
1. Yes Divisible by 2 and 3
2. Yes Last digit is 0
3. Yes 4 x 2 = 8; 22 – 8 =14; 14 is divisible by 7
4. No Divisible by 2 but not by 3
5. Yes Last digit is 5

Activity 152 (p. 78)
1. a, b **2.** a, b, c **3.** c
4. none **5.** a **6.** a

Activity 153 (p. 79)
1. none **2.** a, b **3.** none
4. c **5.** a **6.** a, b, c

Activity 154 (p. 79)
1. 1,144; 5,136; 4,232; 2,200
2. 2,224; 9,176; 1,104; 6,208
3. 3,136; 25,208; 4,160
4. 5,112; 12,120; 17,136; 6,128
Answers will vary.

Activity 155 (p. 80)
1. 1,224; 4,131; 8,802
2. 252; 43,290; 99,333
3. 7,578; 315; 891; 41,319
4. 54; 81
Answers will vary.

Activity 156 (p. 80)
1. 108; 5,301
2. 639; 23,454; 89,136; 9,207
3. 68,895; 72
4. 117; 5,202; 720; 90
Answers will vary.

Activity 157 (p. 81)

1. 4,490; 8,300; 3,520
2. 200; 5,290; 670
3. 7,590; 130; 705,290
4. 110; 6,210; 70

Answers will vary.

Activity 158 (p. 81)

1. Yes Last 3 digits are divisible by 8 ($152 \div 8 = 19$)
2. Yes Sum of the digits (9) is divisible by 9
3. Yes Last digit is 0
4. Yes Last 3 digits are divisible by 8 ($104 \div 8 = 13$)
5. No Sum of digits (19) is not divisible by 9

Activity 159 (p. 82)

1. a, c	**2.** b	**3.** c
4. a, b	**5.** a, b, c	**6.** none

Activity 160 (p. 82)

1. a, b, c	**2.** none	**3.** c
4. a, c	**5.** a	**6.** a, c